PRAISE FOR ADDICT CHICK

"Buckle up and hold on! *Addict Chick unCaged* is a page-turning, incredibly honest, and brilliantly documented memoir about addiction and recovery."

- **Lorelie Rozzano**, Author of *Jagged Little Edges*

"Expertly and uniquely written, *unCaged* is a riveting rollercoaster ride that will keep you up all night. Amanda brings out the badass in us all."

– **Dr. Cali Estes**, The Celebrity Addictions Coach

"We laugh with her. We cry with her. We see ourselves in her. We leave more empowered than we came."

Jennifer Gimenez, Rehab with Dr. Drew

"Soulful and daring, Amanda proves that there is power in telling your story. On every level—this book is remarkable."

– **Blake E. Cohen**, Author of *I Love You, More*

Unquestionably an essential read for women in early recovery. And it's ok that you don't know how to pronounce anonymity—nobody does."

Tim Ryan, A&E's Dope Man

ADDICT CHICK unCaged

AMANDA MEREDITH

Copyright © 2020 by Amanda Meredith

All rights reserved.

No part of this book may be reproduced in any form or by any electronic or mechanical means, including information storage and retrieval systems, without written permission from the author, except for the use of brief quotations in a book review. Sharing any part of the author's writing without giving her credit is theft of her intellectual property. For permission requests, write to the address below or send a message on Facebook

IBSN 978-1-7361431-0-0 | 978-1-7361431-1-7 eBook

Library of Congress Control Number: 2020923000

This book is a memoir. It reflects my present recollections of experiences over time. Some names and characteristics have been changed, some events have been compressed, and some dialogue, events, and letters have been recreated. *Addict Chick unCaged* is a book of memory, and memory has its own story to tell, but I have done my best to make it tell a truthful story. On occasion, I have taken very small liberties with chronology because that is my right as an American.

Mental health and substance use disorder are serious health conditions and require professional medical care. This book is not intended as a substitute for the medical advice of physicians. The author is not a doctor, nor does she claim to be. The author, publisher, and any person, program, or company mentioned anywhere in this book are not responsible or liable for any damage allegedly arising from the reading of this book.

Book cover design by Daniel Flagel | Photography by Mason Meredith | Author photograph by Kim Poole | Poetry of Casey Gallop Stowe used with her permission.

1890 Star Shoot Pkwy Ste 170 #403 | Lexington, KY 40509

www.AddictChick.com

DEDICATED TO MY BEST FRIENDS

Casey Gallop Stowe
Soul sister. Secret keeper. Praying best friend.

Kimberly Louise Poole
For the times we laughed together, cried together, got crazy together, and all the times in between. Best friends forever.

The Addict Chicks
Whose love and badassary brings
magic to my fingertips every single day.

I am the addict that will help pull you from the flames because I am the addict that once crawled out of the fire.

— Addict Chick

CONTENTS

Acknowledgments   xi

Foreword   xvii
Jennifer Gimenez

Introduction   xxi

1. The Letter   1
2. Rehab Dropout   10
3. The Green Key Tag   23
4. The Call   42
5. Active Addiction   51
6. Dope Sex   84
7. Mothers, Daughters, and Sons   92
8. Motherhood   108
9. Test of Wills   118
10. Church Basements   130
11. The Little Book of Addict Chick   144
12. Lonely AF   151
13. Relapse   157
14. Authorship   166
15. Trading the Spoon for the Fork   174
16. Year One   179
17. Childhood Trauma   192
18. Literary Laureate   197
19. Full Circle   200
20. Manteo, North Carolina—2016   224
21. Badass Chicks   236

About Addict Chick   243

ACKNOWLEDGMENTS

Without the support of these badass people,
unCaged would still be Caged.

Will and Lois Poole
Trish Jenkins
Tracy Ward
Tracy Spencer
Tish Chlad
Tina Warner
Tina Smith
Tiffany Montanye
Tessa and Jaz Bare
Teri Lancaster
Tara Flerchinger
Tammy Brooks
Sierra Temple
Shanna Johnson

Shannon Francisco
Sara Hollar
Sandy Badner
Ryan Ely
Roxanne Spencer
Roger Frankham
Robin Smith
Robby Pearson
Pauline Thomas
Nitya Sivakumar
Monica Urzua
Monica Comeaux Cradeur
Mann Mortgage
Lorne Peterson
Lori Wolf
Livvy Jamison
Leslie mills
Leah Cortes
Lance Manka
Kristina Miller
Krista Turner
Kimberly Thompson
Kelly Baummer
Kaylee Moreno
Katie Grady-Gangwer
Katelynn Zimmerle
Kaitlynn Donna Lien.
Kaitlyn McCurday
Julynn Trota
Julieann Beaulieu
Joseph Williams

Jimmy Saxton
Jill Amaya
Jessica Lemp
Jennifer McCann
Jennifer Elfstrom
Jenn Zwickel
Heather Moore
Heather Annette Angle
Gary & Diane Giannoni
Diane's Mom
Crystal Gegenheimer
Courtney Kirlin
Cliff Lowdenback
Christina Odom
Catherine Morris
Catherine Harbert
Brittany Williams
Brandi Montagne
Brandi Miller
Becki Holcomb
Autumn Locascio
Ashley Warden
Ashley Dunn
Amy Jesse
Alicia Wilson-Garcia
Aaron, Brian, and Michael Willman

God, thank you for not throwing in the towel, for keeping me clean, and for the conviction you poured into me before I published another book that I would have to explain when I got up there.

MASON, I'M A KEWL MOM, SO I DON'T KNOW WHY YOU DON'T WANT TO HANG OUT WITH ME. ALSO. I'M NOT DEDICATING ANY MORE BOOKS TO YOU UNTIL YOU CLEAN YOUR ROOM. I LOVE YOU, KID.

MOM, YOUR LONG DEDICATION IS IN CHAPTER TWENTY-ONE, BUT THANK YOU FOR MAKING ME CONFRONT MY PAST AND THEN ENCOURAGING ME TO WRITE ABOUT IT.

KIMBERLY POOLE, FROM D.A.R.E AND THE FUTURE BUSINESS LEADERS OF AMERICA TO ADDICTS AND TWELVE-STEP MEETINGS, FROM CLOVIS, CA TO LEXINGTON, KY, AND A MILLION MEMORIES, TEN THOUSAND INSIDE JOKES, AND HUNDREDS OF MILES OF WALKING TEMPEST AND SULLY BETWEEN US—OUR LIFELONG FRIENDSHIP IS ONE OF THE GREATEST GIFTS OF MY LIFE. THANK YOU FOR READING EVERY DRAFT, MAKING ME LAUGH WHEN I WANTED TO CRY, AND FOR DOOR DASHING DINNER BECAUSE I FORGOT TO EAT. YOU BELIEVED IN ME WHEN I WAS TOO EXHAUSTED TO BELIEVE IN MYSELF, KEPT ME GOING WHEN I WANTED TO QUIT AND MADE SURE THE REST OF MY LIFE DIDN'T FALL APART WHILE I WAS WRITING FIFTEEN HOURS A DAY. THIS BOOK LITERALLY WOULD NOT HAVE BEEN POSSIBLE WITHOUT YOU. CAN WE PLEASE GET SOME GRAETER'S ICE CREAM?

SAMUEL KESARIS, YOU GAVE ME MY FIRST REAL JOB AFTER I GOT CLEAN, AND THAT OPPORTUNITY CHANGED MY ENTIRE LIFE. THANK YOU FOR GIVING ME TIME OFF FROM WORK TO FINISH THE BOOK AND FOR YOUR SUPPORT IN GETTING IT ACROSS THE FINISH LINE. I'LL PROBABLY BE WORKING FOR YOU FOR THE REST OF MY LIFE, SO I'M GLAD THAT YOU'RE SUCH AN EXCEPTIONAL BOSS AND A GREAT GUY. THANK YOU FOR BRINGING KIMMY ASSALONE INTO MY LIFE—I LOVE HER EVEN MORE THAN I LOVE YOU.

Ryan Howard, remember how we used to have big parties at the Gianonni's? Those long summer days and wild nights seem like a lifetime ago now, but they are still some of my favorite memories. We were so young back then—I never in a million years could have imagined the lives we would go on to have. Thank you for backing the book—I am forever grateful. P.S. By the way, the Gio's know *everything*.

Marc Strohmaier, thank you for the late-night chats, pep talks, and support. You have a story of your own, and I think you should write about it.

Tim Wirtala, without you, Addict Chick would have been shut down for copyright violations years ago. Thank you for your friendship, advice, and helping me build a brand that I'm proud of.

Daniel Flagel, book designer, and graphic artist genius—thank you for helping me before I even hired you, for not quitting when I lost my mind over fonts, and for rescuing the book from Photoshop hell. The next time I'm in Argentina, I'll buy you dinner.

Alex Kempsell, my editor and the reason I was saved from grammatical embarrassment—thank you for ripping apart the manuscript, saving me from my liberal use of exclamation points, and teaching me more than I ever wanted to know about narrative tenses. I'll never write another book without you.

My dog park family, Autumn & Khan, Emma, Jan & Angel,

Tiara & Stanley, Jeremy & Taz, Pat, Jack & Jolene, Rita & Bella, Stephen & Lobo, Paul & Brody, Vince, Bruno, and Reagan, you will never know how much you changed my life. Kim, Sully, and I love you! Tempest does not love your dogs.

My Addict Chick family, you are the heartbeat of my recovery—thank you for the years of support. I honor all the addicts that came before me, suffering through their own nightmares, but made it to the other side. Keep up the good fight.

For all the **badass chicks** in my life, check out chapter twenty-one.

Ivey, I love you.

FOREWORD
JENNIFER GIMENEZ

Everybody thinks they want to write a book until they sit down in front of a blank piece of paper and try to write a book. It takes a ton of commitment, effort, and determination to finish a manuscript. I'm a feature writer for *Recovery Today Magazine*, and every month I'm challenged with writing a few thousand words. So, I can only imagine how hard it is to write eighty thousand. Being asked to write the foreword to a book is a big responsibility because the author trusts you to introduce the work they have poured their hearts into—it's like their baby. So I was honored when Amanda asked me to write the foreword for *unCaged*.

The first connection I had with Amanda was on Facebook. We had many mutual friends, and they often shared quotes that she had written. I could tell that we both stood for the same values as women in recovery, and I thought her writing was fearless, honest, and highly relatable. Not long after, I was introduced to her by my husband, Tim Ryan, and our connection was immediate. I naturally gravitate towards strong, positive women, and Amanda is beautiful both on the inside and out. She is a fighter, a survivor, and one badass chick. She has turned the trials and mistakes of her past into a powerful comeback story. Recovery brought us together, but a shared passion for helping people find freedom is what makes us friends.

At the age of thirteen, I was discovered by a photographer in Hollywood, and it wasn't long before fame, drugs, and alcohol consumed my life. I've been sober since January 15th, 2006, and have devoted my life to fighting the stigma associated with substance abuse.

Recently, I had the opportunity to share my own story of addiction during a TEDx event. While preparing for my appearance, I had to confront parts of my past that brought back some rather traumatic memories. It was gut-wrenching to relive the worst aspects of my life, and I struggled with baring my soul in front of cameras and a live audience. I was terrified but realized that my fear was holding me back. With the support of some amazing people, I got on that stage and unleashed all my fears and pain. The process freed me; sharing my story and being vulnerable helped me heal. I imagine Amanda feels the same way about writing the story of her life and sharing it with the world.

Addict Chick unCaged was written five years after the release of Amanda's first book, *Addict Chick: Sex, Drugs, & Rock 'N Roll*, and takes readers beyond life in active addiction and into a life lived without the use of drugs. Writing comes less from the mind and more from the soul, and she does a phenomenal job of describing the challenges women face during early recovery. I believe that even those who haven't struggled with substance abuse will find pieces of themselves in her story. Most women have had their hearts broken, battled with body image issues, or experienced childhood trauma. It's been a long time since I've read such a gutsy, bold, and courageous book.

In early recovery, I was told that it was necessary to find my voice. Even more importantly, once I found it, I needed to have it heard. Amanda has definitely found her voice. It's my pleasure to introduce you to *Addict Chick unCaged*. You're going to love this book. Happy reading!

xoxo, JG
October 2020 | Beverly Hills, CA.

Jennifer Gimenez is one of the nation's leading addiction recovery advocates, and with over 14 years of sobriety in Hollywood, she is one badass chick!

She has appeared on over 100 magazine covers and rocked out in the music videos of Mick Jagger, Prince, 2Pac, Lionel Richie, and many more. Her film credits include *Blow* with Johnny Depp, *Vanilla Sky* with Tom Cruise, *Charlie's Angels*, and the Oscar-nominated documentary, *Let's Get Lost*.

She has starred in the TV Shows, Sober House, Celebrity Rehab, Rehab with Dr. Drew, and The Real Housewives of Beverly Hills. She is an expert guest on CNN, The Today Show, Inside Edition, ENews, The View, and The Doctors TV Show.

INTRODUCTION

This book contains scenes that include drug addiction, IV drug use, childhood sexual abuse, trauma, and is sexually graphic. I extend this warning so that those who wish to avoid these subjects may make an informed decision about whether to continue reading.

I want to offer the following statements in the spirit of transparency, honesty, and the desire not to be tyrannized for sharing my story and experiences therein. My actions are in no way a reflection of any of the twelve-step programs that exist in over 170 countries worldwide. The very last thing I want to do is turn anybody off a path that might save their life. I am not a recovery expert and have never claimed to be. I do not have the magical spell for getting you off dope, to sober you up, or to make you stop eating at Krispy Kreme.

Over my years on social media and with the release of my first book, I have received substantive criticisms, some with validity—

Introduction

but most from people being judgy—over how I choose to recover. I (mostly) don't give a damn. The stigma is alive, silence kills, and if my story can inspire even one person to get their shit together, then I'm good.

My beliefs, thoughts, and opinions are based solely on my individual experience. I support all roads that lead to recovery. My story is not your story, so neither is my recovery. Recovery is unique to each person, and there is no straight path we can all follow to get there. I truly believe that even though some of us are further down the road than others, we are all the same distance from the gutter.

Please understand that your opinion on how I live my life only matters if you're my mama or Jesus.

1
THE LETTER

Excerpt from *Addict Chick: Sex, Drugs, & Rock 'N Roll*

I loved him so much that I would have died for him.

And then I did.

He was beautiful, the sexiest man I had ever met. I mean, the second I saw him, I just wanted to rip my clothes off and beg him to take me to bed. His bad-boy charisma dripped off his sexy hard body. His hair was golden brown and cut short to his head. His green eyes were clear and could change colors based on his moods. They were soft when he was happy but could flash green fire when he was pissed.

His hands were big and rough, exactly the way a man's hands should be. And when he touched my body with them, nothing in the world ever felt better.

He was tall, well over six feet. His body was ripped, with sinewy muscles packed onto his perfect frame. Really, he had muscles in places that I didn't even know that they existed. He was so strong that he could pick me up and toss me into the air like I was a doll.

His sexy crooked smile framed perfect white teeth, and he could take me from sad to blissfully happy, instantly. Sometimes he would bite his lower lip, and it would transform his menacing exterior into that of a sweet and vulnerable boy. But he wasn't a boy; he was all man and a walking wet dream.

His name was Cage, and I loved him like the Wind.

I drop the loose change onto the counter, and the sound echoes through the silent house. I pull out her wallet right as my mom walks into the room. Her eyes fall on the contents of her purse, currently in a messy pile on her kitchen counter.

"What are you looking for?" she asks suspiciously.

"The same thing I've been getting out of this big piece of luggage every day since I got home," I sigh. "Your keys, so I can check the mail. Don't worry, I didn't steal any money and all your quarters are still there."

She flinches, pain crossing her face. I instantly feel guilty as we stare at each other over the granite-covered island, and know that we're both thinking about the same thing. The memory pulls at my brain, and I wish I had kept my mouth shut. What I did to her was despicable, but I do not have time to learn any life lessons right now.

I did terrible things to my mom during my addiction to meth and stolen from her so often that I can't even remember all the things I took. But I'll never forget how badly I had hurt her when I robbed her of something that wasn't even worth much—not in cash anyway.

For months she had been collecting the newly minted quarters, one for each of the fifty states. She wanted to give a set to each of her children and grandchildren at Christmas that year. Every week, she would painstakingly go through her change, searching for the quarters she still needed to complete a set. My mom had special-ordered books to organize each collection of quarters and purchased enough for everybody. Sometimes, I would watch as she discovered a quarter she didn't have, pull out one of the books, and carefully place it in the correct spot. I knew it meant a lot to her, but that didn't stop me from breaking her heart anyway.

One day, when I knew she wasn't home, I snuck in through the doggy door of her house. Crawling inside, I headed straight to her office and opened the cabinet where she kept the books. I pulled out each completed set, and one by one, popped out every quarter, letting them fall to the ground. Generously, I left the top book intact. Mostly because there were only a few quarters in there, but also so my mom wouldn't notice that the others were now empty.

She did.

"Out of everything you could steal from me, why would you take the quarter books?" she asked, tears swimming in her eyes and the betrayal clear on her face.

In what had then become second nature to me, I responded with vehement and vicious denial. I swore on my life that I hadn't stolen her stupid quarters. I screamed hateful things as she broke down and cried in front of me. How dare she accuse me of being a thief? As I watched her sob, I told her that I hated her and that she was an awful mother. And then, feeling nothing but offended, I went to buy dope with the stolen quarters, leaving her crying on the floor.

Remembering that day is too much. Guilt slams into me, and I handle the moment all wrong.

"This is ridiculous!" I say in a hard and unyielding voice. "It's been well over a month since I last got high. I haven't stolen anything. You need to start trusting me."

It's mostly true. The only thing I've stolen since I got home is her extra pair of tweezers, perfectly normal behavior for a daughter when it comes to her mom's beauty products. I mean, she kind of signed up for that shit when she gave birth to a girl.

I hear metal slide across granite as she scoops her keys up off the counter and passes them to me. "Why is a letter from him so important to you?" she asks. "He destroyed your life. Don't you think you should move on and forget about him?"

I don't say anything as I palm the keys and walk back to my room. I can feel her disappointment follow me across the silence, but I keep my mouth shut. She doesn't understand; there's no possible way she can. There's nothing I can say that will make her get it, and I don't want to fight with her or argue; we've done enough of both over the last few years.

Slipping on my shoes, I feel my adrenaline start to race. Today will be the day; I can sense it in my soul, and I can feel it between my legs. I practically skip out the front door. Cutting across the grass, I barely notice the neighbors across the street as they look up and stare at me. They probably wonder if I'm still on drugs. I jump inside my little black VW and nearly jump right back out.

My ass is on fire. The seats are blisteringly hot, and I wiggle around, trying to ease the sting. The Texas sun is fierce, no matter the time of year. As soon as I start the engine, I blast the AC, not caring that it's blowing hot air straight into my face.

I turn my radio, slip my car into first gear, and head towards town. It's a beautiful day, the sun is bright, and there isn't a cloud in the sky. Smiling, I rev the engine and feel the power beneath me. I lower my window and lose my breath as the cool air rushes in and surrounds me—the same way Cage did.

I slow down as I approach the main intersection in the tiny town of Whitehouse, Texas. Kids lined the street, waiting at the crosswalk and for parents to scoop them up. School had just been let out, and the last thing I needed was a ticket for speeding in a school zone. My mom would kill me.

When I see the cop pull up beside me, I feel panicky. My first reaction is to wonder where in the car I had stashed my dope. Relief floods me when I remember that I'm clean, and there aren't any drugs in my vehicle. It looks like I won't be going to jail tonight.

The light turns green, so I continue down the busy street and turn into the post office, parking right in front. Jumping out of the car, I quickly make my way to the entrance. A sweet old-timer holds the door open for me.

"Thanks, babe," I wink at him, and he smiles back at me.

I make a beeline for the box marked 902, and after fumbling with my keys for a second, I slide the key into the slot. Feeling my breath quicken, I open the small metal door, and I'm instantly irritated. The box is jammed full, crap wedged into every corner. It's a struggle, but with some determination, I finally pull everything free.

Slipping my haul under my arm, I lock the box and walk to the sorting table. I toss all the bullshit advertisements and junk mail right into the recycling bin. I pull out the magazines one by one and stare at them; *HGTV, The Family Handyman, Fine Woodworking, People*, and about twenty other rags that my mom doesn't need. Organizing them into a pile, I roll my eyes and mutter, "Mom needs to calm down with these subscriptions."

I'm left with a thick stack of envelopes; *the good stuff.* My fingers start flicking them forward, eyes searching for the only one that matters. My disappointment grows as they fall until I reach the very last envelope. There it was, my name, written in Cage's hand. Excitement floods me as I dance out the door and back to my car.

Tossing everything but his letter into the passenger seat, I run my fingers across the envelope. His hands had touched this paper, and his tongue had licked the band to seal it. I feel a tingle between my legs as I rip open the envelope. Four pages fall out, and I notice that one of them contains a drawing. I pull it out, my eyes sweep across the page, and my heart drops.

In a time before our lives were consumed by drugs and chasing dope, Cage and I spent afternoons at the park near my house. We would bring blankets and spread them out near the pond where the ducks swam. Spreading out beneath a beautiful weeping willow tree, we lounged around for hours. I would prop my head on his lap and rotate between reading, napping, and watching him.

Sketch pad on his lap, his hands would move across the paper, lost in whatever he was drawing. Usually, it was me. Although he was extremely gifted, I always felt strange when I saw his pictures of me.

"You nailed my hair, the shape of my face, and my big nose," I would point out, "but that doesn't exactly look like me. That chick is beautiful."

"I draw you the way that I see you, silly," he would say before planting a kiss on my forehead.

Those words come back to haunt me now. I look down at the piece of paper and watch my hand tremble. Tears burn my eyes, and my lower lip quivers. Roughly, I pull my arm across my face, stopping the tears before they can spill over.

It's a picture of me, and I do not look beautiful; I don't even look ugly. I look depraved and twisted. *This is how he sees me now.* I felt sick as my eyes sweep across the page.

Drawn in black ink, I'm splayed across the white paper; back arched and legs bent at the knees. I am utterly naked except for the thigh-high fishnet stockings and garter belt. No panties. Cage had drawn a little landing strip of hair in the divide between my legs.

That detail makes me pause; he had always wanted me to be waxed clean down there. He insisted, and I complied. So, every four weeks, I would be tortured by some random woman sent from hell to humiliate me. She would make me spread my legs, get on my knees, pull my butt cheeks apart, smear hot wax from front to back, and rip out every piece of hair—effectively taking my pride with them.

Forcing my eyes across the image, I try not to flinch. My hands are cupped beneath my breasts, pushing them towards my face. Round and huge, they are not proportionate to the rest of my body. They look like they are rising from the page, reaching for something. I quickly glance up to see what it is.

The drawing's thin lips are wide open, and my tongue is twisted, diving down toward my breasts. Spit drips off my chin. Or maybe that was meant to be blood; we had exchanged plenty of both during our relationship. He had covered each of my nipples with a big X that he roughly shaded in.

Clearly, he remembers the times we played that game during nights of drunken sex. Back then, he had used black masking tape to brand me. Cage would tear off pieces and cross them over my tits. He liked to stare into my eyes and rip them off as he moved between my legs. My screams of pain only excited him more. I could see heat flash in his green eyes as I whimpered and begged.

Even though I had never craved pain in my sex, I loved these games just as much as he did because I lived to please him. I would do anything to make him happy, even if that meant I had to change who I was.

But now, looking at this picture, all I want to do is stab him in his black heart.

In the picture, I'm lying on a pile of chains, the metal twisting in mounds beneath me. My wrists and ankles are bound and secured with locks that run toward a steel ring hanging high above my head. He has tethered a leash to the ring, like a dog leash, with spikes running its length. My eyes follow it until it disappears behind my head. The leash is connected to the back of the thick collar he has drawn around my neck. If he'd had color pencils in prison, I know that the collar would have been bright red; the color of hate.

The word WHORE is written across my throat in big, block letters.

There it was; the real reason he sent this to me. His message. His way of showing me how he feels about me. He had drawn me precisely the way he sees me now. I'm quick with my words, but Cage is a master at delivering his rage with just a picture.

The only thing he got right was my eyes. Round, wide, and full of tears, I can see the shame of who he thinks I've become and the regret for what we will never be again. Fury and bitterness spill out of me, and I toss the drawing to the floor.

Choking back a sob I can barely contain, I pick up the rest of the letter. Turning the pages over slowly in my hand, I consider not reading it. I already know that Cage's words will deliver more torment to my already broken soul, but I read it anyway.

And immediately respond to the motherfucker.

2

REHAB DROPOUT

Cage,

I got your letter and the porn you drew for me. Not sure if that was supposed to be me, but you missed the mark. I could see how being in prison, surrounded by men all day, would have you slipping.

    I'm not proud of how I behaved when I was getting high and chasing dope, but I'm clean now. I know that you don't believe me and I really don't care. I suppose if you expect nothing but the worst from me, why should I expect anything better from you?

    It's easy to get clean in jail, far more difficult to make the conscious choice to enter treatment and then actually do it. You said you know me better than anybody, but suddenly I feel like you don't know me, and maybe you never did. If you did, you would believe that I can go the rest of my life without a relapse. I'm not strong enough to stay clean? Baby, you either never realized it or have forgotten, but I do not fail. Not with anything. I'll stay clean.

Yes, I screwed up and made mistakes, but every single one of them was when I was on drugs. Before dope, you know that no woman in the world has ever loved a man the way I loved you; I lived to make you happy.

Don't forget that this all happened because YOU decided to get high the first time. As far as I'm concerned, YOU are lucky that I even attempted to allow you into MY space again.

Go fuck yourself,

Amanda

Spent from my rage writing, I drop the phone into my lap and let my head fall back against the car seat. I feel the hot tears flowing down my face like rivers of fire. My thoughts are firmly planted in hell, and I feel like I'll be stuck here forever. With as little as one letter and one drawing, Cage broke me all over again. His words cutting like a razor blade across my heart, I can feel his hate drip like ice water into my soul.

Having spent years numbing myself with drugs, the sudden rush of emotions manifests itself with a physical reaction. Wrenching forward, I puke right into my lap.

Great, I think, as I stare down at the disgusting mess. I watch as the tears drop from my face and pool with the vomit. Overcome with grief and anger; I feel a war begin to surge inside my spirit.

A battle between the woman I'm fighting to be and the drug addict I used to be.

I'm crippled with emotions I don't want to feel, and in a place I never thought I would be. I want to burn the world down with Cage inside of it. I want to rage at how unfair this all was. I want to scream until my voice is gone. And I want to crawl into Cage's lap and beg him to fix this and make it okay.

The soul inside my physical body is trying to crawl out of my chest and into my head. My thoughts race towards the darkness because it wasn't very long ago that that's where I would go to escape the hell my life had become. And at this moment, the only thing I want is relief.

My subconscious has been waiting for an opportunity for my resolve to weaken, and now it has. My thoughts twist together, humming between my ears. The voice, the one I hadn't heard since getting clean, slips to the center of my focus, and I reach for it. It spreads through my mind, calming me down. It's familiar and comforting, so I lean into it and let it take me.

I close my eyes and let my memories lull me back to a time when feeling nothing was so much easier than feeling everything.

When the only thing that mattered—the only thing I needed—was a syringe full of dope and a good vein.

My vision dances back to the ritual of filling my needle with crystals, beautiful rocks that I had willingly sold my soul for.

My soul! My eyes fly open.

Just over a month ago, I begged God to save me in this same post office parking lot. And He did. I mean, I hadn't gotten high since that moment. I know I should be reaching for Jesus right now to bring me back from the thoughts that I know I shouldn't be having, but I can't. I'm paralyzed by this consuming desire to ease the pain that Cage delivered straight to my broken heart. My longing to plunge a needle deep into the first available vein roars through me, and I feel like I will choke on the hate that is raging inside my heart.

Hate for myself, contempt for the power Cage had over me, and disdain for the love that I couldn't stop feeling for him. He doesn't believe that I went to rehab or that I've stayed clean. And it drives me insane that he called me a liar. I refuse to acknowledge, even to myself, that he has every right to feel the way he does. While he rotted behind bars, I made promises I never kept, did every terrible thing I swore I would never do, and had spent the last four years lying my ass off.

I'm telling the truth now, I scream inside my head.

I've been home from rehab for over a week, and I haven't gotten high once. Every day I'm torn between wanting to rush into the world, proudly presenting myself as this tough chick who has overcome a powerful addiction and being too chickenshit to leave for fear that I would fall right off the wagon.

Seriously, there are moments that I stand in the shower, crying and wondering if I am going to be able to do this. I try so hard not to think about it, but I can't help it. I know that it has been a long time since I loved being high or loved the way it made me feel, but damn, I hate the way I feel without it too. Staying clean for the rest of my life seems impossible, and I can't imagine anybody being able to do it. And if nobody else can, how will I?

In my mind, I know what will happen if I relapse; I'll lose Mason forever, my mom will break apart, and I will be dead in a few years—maybe even sooner, if I kill myself first. It's strange that even knowing all that, I still think about getting high.

I have tons of support, a family that loves me, and God looking out for me, but ultimately? I think it will come down to the strength of will that exists somewhere within the woman I am. And I pray that woman is strong enough.

But so far, I am still clean. I have even stayed away from all my friends. Friends that I was getting high with shortly before I left for rehab. Deep down, if I'm honest with myself, I know that if I see them, I will soon be using *with* them. If they talk me into getting high or offer me dope, it won't be my fault if I relapsed, and somewhere in the part of my brain that is still sick, I'm planning my relapse.

I would like to say that my choice to hide away is all my own, but in truth, my mom put a tracker on my phone; if she catches me at the lake or anywhere I wasn't supposed to be, it's game over.

When I was in treatment, I heard another patient say, "The worst thing that can ever happen to an addict is when our parents discover Al-Anon or Nar-Anon or some other support group."

He wasn't bullshitting because while I was getting clean, my mama was busy finding some recovery of her own. She put together a list of boundaries and rules, deal-breakers that I had to follow, or she would completely cut me off. She even wrote them down like a contract. As she read them to me, I tried not to get mad, but some of them were utterly ridiculous.

"I have to leave the bathroom door open?" I asked incredulously.

"Yes," she replied, "so you can't hide in there and get high."

Lame, I thought, rolling my eyes, but I kept my mouth shut.

I could tell that she wasn't messing around. I had already been clean for a month, so I didn't think all these rules were necessary, but I did everything she asked me to do. And I felt like I should be getting a gold star or, at the very least, a welcome home party. But my mom was still pissed at me. Like, super pissed, and there would be no party for me.

"What were you thinking?" she yelled at me as I walked through the door on my first day back from treatment.

Jesus, I did not want to be having that conversation. I was exhausted, and I knew that she would ask me questions that I didn't have the answers for. And I had no desire to try and dissect the inner workings of my broken moral compass.

"Mom, stop making this into a bigger deal than it is," I yelled back, louder than I intended.

Swinging one bag across my shoulder, I grabbed my suitcase handle and headed straight to my room. Wheels squeaking over wood floors, I slammed my bedroom door to indicate that our conversation was over.

She is having none of that, and the door flies open.

"No closed doors in this house!" she barked before turning around and disappearing back down the hallway.

Rolling my eyes, I threw myself onto the bed.

God, this is so freaking embarrassing. Flipping onto my stomach, I buried my face into my hands and prayed that the bed would swallow me. It was more than just embarrassing. I had failed, and somehow, it felt even worse than most of the things I had done when I was using drugs.

Just a few days shy of completing treatment, I had gotten kicked out of the program; the one that my mother had spent her retirement on to save my life. Shuddering, I thought about the call I had to make to my mom that day.

"Mom, I'll be home a few days earlier than expected," I had said when she answered, my voice trembling from nerves.

"Why, what's wrong?" I had been able to hear the panic in her voice.

When I told her, the disappointment in her voice was so palpable that I was immediately filled with shame. She didn't understand how I could do what I did, and I couldn't even explain it because I didn't know how I could either.

There's a philosophy called Occam's razor, which I think applies here. This rule states that between two explanations, the simplest one is more likely to be true. I think that in this situation, the simplest explanation is that somebody screwed up. And that somebody was me.

I didn't get booted for relapsing, though that seemed like it would've been a lesser sin than what I had actually done. Maybe even understandable, since relapse appears to be a regular part of recovery for most people. I wonder if they would've kept me if that had been my crime?

But no, I got kicked out because I was weak, completely powerless over my sick desire for physical release. But wasn't lust also an addiction? Apparently, it wasn't a forgivable one.

A million justifications played through my mind while I tried to excuse my behavior. What did they expect would happen? You put a group of men and women together, take away our drugs, and what do we have left? Sex.

Yes, they had made it very clear when I first got there that relationships between patients were not allowed, and you would be removed from the program for the first offense. They even made me sign something stating that I understood the rules. In my defense, though, it was about fifteen hours after my last shot of dope, and I was not in the state of mind to fully appreciate what I was signing. And I don't think they appreciated the fact that I made it a whopping thirty-one days before I had that poor boy on his back in the woods.

Except for one little incident, I had been the ideal patient. Hell, if they had awards, I would've won Patient of the Month! I participated in all the activities, went to all the groups, and did all assigned homework. I was very engaged in my treatment plan and did everything they told me to do.

Except for that one time I did exactly what they told me *not* to do.

He was at least twelve years my junior, and we had been circling each other from the day I had finally emerged from my room. Typically, I don't go after younger guys, but I decided to make an exception because the days were much more exciting with a hot guy to flirt with.

The day before he was scheduled to leave the program, I decided that I needed to have him. It was unacceptable that I hadn't gotten laid in what seemed like a million years, and my last opportunity was about to walk out the door. I don't know what else to tell you. Our foreplay had been going on for weeks, and maybe I needed the excitement that breaking the rules would bring. Besides, I knew I could do it and not get caught.

I should have just banged myself that day, and none of this would have happened.

During our last group of the day, I told him to meet me at the walking trail at the end of the courtyard. The patients were allowed to hike it whenever we had free time, and I had spent many hours walking the winding paths. Though cameras monitored it, I knew there were a few places on the curves that were out of sight.

When he showed up, we took off for the trails, walking quickly. I knew that the techs would note that we were down there together and watch us closely, so we didn't have a lot of time. When we got to the bend in the trail marked by a scarred tree, I pulled him off the path and into the woods. I could tell he was nervous, but I wasn't; I was excited.

Dropping to my knees, I pulled him to the ground and pushed him onto his back. I moved above him and kissed his mouth while reaching for the button on his jeans. To add a visual to my words, I licked my lips and said, "We need to hurry. Take off your pants."

Slipping off my shoes, I quickly pulled off my black yoga pants to free my legs. I kept my thong on because we were in the forest; there were bugs and shit, and I had to push out the thought of an eight-legged spider crawling into my vagina before I changed my mind. Using my legs, I lowered my body onto him, a deep guttural moan escaping my lips as the pressure of him filled me. I had just begun to rock back up when I heard the voices—faint but getting louder. Frustrated, I almost kept going, but the fear of getting caught overrode my desire to cum. Barely.

"Get dressed!" I whispered.

He jumped up and began pulling on his clothes, the panic clear on his face. "What are we going to do?" he asked.

My clumsy ass nearly fell over when I pulled on my pants and tried to shove my feet back into my shoes at the same time. Panting from the effort, I said, "You head back the way we came and if they ask where I am, tell them we split up and have no idea which way I went."

"Where are you going to go, though?"

I shot a quick look up the hill behind me. "I'll figure it out, but for the love of God, do not tell them we hooked up!"

"Okay," he mumbled nervously before turning around and heading towards the approaching voices.

Turning around, I walked deeper into the woods, reasonably sure that I could circle back once I found the fence that ran along the perimeter of the property. I could still hear them calling my name, so I started walking faster. The terrain quickly changed from flat to steep, and I had second thoughts about what I was doing. What if I was wrong and got lost out here? It was getting dark, and I was not what anybody would consider 'outdoorsy.' Thought of getting ripped apart by a bear gave me pause, but then I thought about my mama finding out what I was up to and started hustling double time.

Using my hands, I pulled myself up the side of the hill, trying not to think about the bugs crawling around in the dirt. Dry branches and shrubs grazed against my clothing and scratched the tops of my hands. When I crested the top, I felt pretty damn proud. Then, I turned around to survey my accomplishment and was embarrassed for myself. The very slight incline measured only about a hundred yards; even a toddler could've made it without a problem.

Taking a last look at the sunset that was lingering on the horizon, the orange glow peeking through the trees, I turned around and headed in the direction that I *thought* was the right way.

After a few minutes, I came to a small, barbed wire fence. My sweatshirt ripped as I crawled beneath it, but I made it to the other side like a champ. Maybe I should join the military. I could see the facility's doors to the right of the lawn's slope. *Boom.* I delivered pizza's in college and always had a pretty good sense of direction—except for the cardinal kind. Please, never include south or east in your directions. I'm better with landmarks like Starbucks and the GPS on my iPhone. However, I did traverse just through a forest without dying, so whatever.

Trying to avoid the cameras, at least the ones I could see, I hugged the stone wall that edges the flower beds and crept towards the bank of windows that lead to my room. I glanced around to make sure nobody was wandering by, then reached for the window closest to me and slid it open. Taking a deep breath, I jumped and tucked my arm over the top of the windowsill. For a second, I just hung there. God, I hope nobody is watching this; I probably look like a crazed sloth hanging from a branch. Swinging my hips back and forth, I threw my right leg up, tucked my heel on the inside of the ledge, and pulled myself into a straddle position.

If my ascent had been less than graceful, my descent was a Greek tragedy. I tumbled through the open space, banged my elbow on the dresser, and hit the ground with a hollow thump. My speed date with gravity left me dizzy, but I shook it off and quickly shed my clothes, kicking them under the bed. I was just slipping under my comforter when Kat, my favorite tech, walked into the room.

"Where have you been?" she asked, her eyes sweeping around the room.

I tried to fake a yawn and ended up sounding like a baby bird with dysentery. "What do you mean? I'm in bed."

"Weren't you just out walking the trail?"

"I was, but I came back because I was tired," I lied.

She squinted suspiciously, and the silence that dropped between us was so taut that I almost confessed right then.

Giving me a last look, she said, "Well, okay. Have a good night."

As soon as the door closed, I smiled. I couldn't believe we had gotten away with it, and I felt like freaking Macgyver. I mean, if anybody needed me to defuse a bomb with a paperclip and duct tape, I'd be on it.

Without a worry in the world, I closed my eyes and slept like a baby.

The next morning, before I have even had coffee, I learned that I hadn't been as slick as I thought; there would be very real consequences to my actions.

I was pulled into the admissions office and could tell by the grim look on my counselor's face that she knew what I had been doing in the woods.

Before she even opened her mouth, I had a complete meltdown.

"Please, it's not what you think!"

She shook her head with disappointment. "We've reviewed the videos and know everything."

I was both mortified and ashamed, but mostly, I was scared.

"I'm truly sorry. I made a mistake! Please don't make me leave," I begged, panic swelling and making me feel like I was going to puke.

"You knew the rules, and you decided to break them. I'm sorry, but we have to ask you to leave."

"I'm not ready! If you kick me out, I'm going to get high!" I threatened, tears falling hot and fast down my face.

But no amount of pleading and crying would change their minds. I had to leave the program that I was sure had saved my life. I had banged my way right out of the chance to finish what I had started, and it was entirely my fault.

The smell of the bile in my lap brings me back to the present.

As my body begs for relief, I realize that I have a choice. The outcome of my entire future comes down to the decision I make at this moment—a choice between living and dying. I can run back to the dope game and become everything Cage still thinks I am, or I can harden up and be the badass chick that I know I am.

Determination fueling my resolve, I pull myself together. I am going to stay clean, just to prove that bastard wrong.

3

THE GREEN KEY TAG

*I*t's barely noon, and it's already been one hell of a day inside my mind. I haven't gotten out of bed or even left my room. Buried beneath cotton sheets and a black comforter, I have been lying here for hours. I didn't sleep for shit and should be dead ass tired, but my brain won't be quiet. And I can't garner up any sensation that remotely resembles an emotion. I stare up at the ceiling and wish I could feel something—anything.

I should have been so excited when I woke up this morning; the sun was shining, and the temperatures were starting to feel like spring. I have loved this time of year since I was a little girl. Cold weather giving way to spring means that summer wasn't far behind, and summer means BBQs, swimming, and flip flops with the promise of good times and summer love. And it means that winter is over.

I hate the winter, but I especially loathed it when I was strung out and homeless. I will probably dread every winter for the rest of my life, remembering how cold it was to sleep in my car. Even with piles of blankets I had stolen from my mom's house, I would shiver so hard that the vibrations from my own body would rock me to sleep.

Pulling the blanket tighter around me, I roll over in bed and stare out the window. I can see the squirrels racing up and down the trees, intent on stuffing their fat cheeks full of the treats my mom hangs from every corner of her yard. I love watching the squirrels; I have spent hours on my mom's back porch, totally enthralled with the rodents. But for some reason, I cannot manifest even the smallest hint of joy inside of myself. I can't feel anything—it's like I'm dead inside.

Since getting clean, I've felt like I am two different people trapped inside one body, and I have no idea how to cope with the never-ending emotional roller coaster. One moment it feels like World War III has started inside my soul as every damn emotion I've ever felt slams into me all at once. And in the next moment, I feel paralyzed and unable to feel anything, even when I know I should be feeling something. It's immensely frustrating and utterly exhausting.

And the onslaught comes during the most random times and in the oddest situations. I will feel a rush of blinding anger at my mom for not buying me the ice cream that I liked but let the idiot that cut me off in the parking lot roll by without so much the honk of my horn.

Since putting down the dope, I have completed thirty days of rehab, including therapy and a ton of knowledge about what I would be facing in the coming months. Even before I got clean, I researched recovery from meth addiction, sure that I would find an easy solution or magic pill for getting off meth. I would pour over blogs and articles as I cruised around Google, searching for hours. Of course, nearly every report said that the first step in getting clean would be actually to stop getting high. Well, duh.

I didn't find that helpful or interesting. Part of me was hoping that I would come across some enlightening piece of literature that would teach me how to continue to get high and enjoy the unlimited amounts of energy and sex without burning the rest of my life to the ground.

No such article exists because it is not possible. No human on earth has ever managed a drug addiction without significant damage to everything else they love. Those that don't agree just haven't gotten there yet, but they'll find themselves in the same dark place as the rest of us.

One of the most compelling articles talked about something called The Wall. It's a period between thirty and ninety days into recovery in which addicts are most vulnerable to relapse. It's also the reason so many people say that meth addiction is not treatable. People find no pleasure in life during this time, so the cravings to get high become overwhelming.

And here we are.

Nothing that I learned, read, been told, or previously knew to be true could have prepared me for what the months after getting clean would be like. One moment I was flying high, giddy on my recovery, and the next moment I wanted to get high more than I wanted to live. And every emotion that did hit me felt artificial, like I was only feeling it because I knew I was supposed to—kind of like a placebo.

My mind slips back to a place that I try so hard to push out of my head, but in my desperation to feel something, I let them come. Anything, just to feel, even if it's a memory of a life I will never have again.

I find comfort in knowing that I can recall the memories even if I can't find escape through a needle in my arm. It's like the thoughts of how I felt on meth are never far away. They're just waiting in the shadows until I am vulnerable. And as soon as I am, they come flooding back, eager to drown me. As I lie in the cotton cocoon of my bed, I open myself up to the memories and let them take me.

I imagine filling up a rig with those beautiful, energy-producing crystals and pulling in just enough water to cover them. They melt into a thick syrup as I shake the needle and turn it over in my hands.

In my memory, I tie off my arm above the crook of my elbow and feel the rush of blood pushing through my body as my heart starts to pump harder. My brain has already found its way back to the part of me that craves the euphoria that a shot would give me. My mouth waters as I feel the confidence and power start to grow inside me. I feel beautiful, sexy, and—damn—I feel invincible.

And then I feel tears falling down my face—scalding hot and flowing like a river through hell. Finally, I feel guilt and shame rise inside me. Not really the emotions I was looking for, but at least I was feeling something.

The psychological warfare that rages inside my soul is enough to make me wonder if dying would be better than this. I am either feeling everything, or I'm feeling nothing. I cannot live without dope, but I also can't live a life that includes getting high every day. I try to remember a time before it was too late—when I lived a normal life—and I can't even conjure up a moment in which that life made sense. The minute-by-minute struggle is unbearable, and I don't think I'm strong enough to do this.

My reverie is broken when my phone rings. Sitting up in bed, I dig around until I find it. My kid is calling, and a smile spreads across my face.

I click the button to accept. "Hey, baby!"

"Hi, mama, when are you going to be here?" he asks. The sound of his sweet little boy voice makes my heart dance.

The feelings I have been begging for finally come—the right ones. I'm flooded with love for this little boy, and I feel genuine happiness and contentment. I was going to get my son back, and there was nothing more important than that.

"Nana and I leave here in about a month, and we are so excited to see you!"

"Are you staying forever this time?"

My heart clenches at the question, and I feel crushing guilt that my son, my only child, must ask me that. And he has every right to ask because I've never stayed before. Usually, it's a visit that lasts a few days, and then I leave him, eager to get back to Texas where I can get high.

I force a smile onto my face so that he can hear it across the thousand miles that separate us. "Kiddo," I say, "I'm moving there for forever. I rented a townhouse that's about five minutes from your dad's. You're going to have your own bedroom and everything."

"Okay. I love you. Bye." He quickly hangs up.

He doesn't believe me. And why should he? After a million broken promises and countless lies, he has no reason to believe anything I say. I have shattered his little heart so often that I'm going to have to spend the rest of my life trying to make up for the damage.

I force my body up and swing my legs over the side of the bed. Catching a glimpse of my wild hair in my dresser mirror, I'm horrified by what I see. *I need to brush that shit out*, I think. Rubbing my hands over my face, I attempt to jump-start my brain.

Tonight is kind of a big deal, and I suddenly feel a little pride creep into my thoughts. With a smile, I stand up and walk across the room to my closet. I have no idea what I'm going to wear, but I know that I want to look hot but classy. Scanning across the sea of t-shirts, dresses, and tank tops, I have a sinking feeling that I probably didn't own anything that matched the outfit I had in my head. My clothing choices were somewhere between hooker and stripper—and not even like fancy Vegas stripper, more like a stripper from 'Time Out,' the old club down on Highway 155.

Even if I was brave enough to wear any of this crap, which I'm not, there isn't a chance in hell that I would be able to fit into any of it. I had gained a pound—or two, or ten—since quitting the meth diet.

Maybe I'll wear some cute shorts. I pull them out one at a time. Narrowing my eyes, I examine each pair and toss them to the floor, disgusted. Even if I could get them over my ever-growing ass, they're so short that the bottom of my buttcheeks would peek out, and there was an excellent chance that the lips of my vagina did too. What was it about meth that inspires women to think they're filming a scene from *The Dukes of Hazzard* every time they get dressed?

No, tonight is very important to me, and I want to look like a chick with a little dignity and respect. I'm not sure how I'll pull it off, considering everything I own just screams skank. Sighing loudly, I slump to the floor and bury my face into my hands, surrounded by piles of shame.

A few moments later, my mom comes strolling into the room. "What's wrong with you?"

"I have nothing to wear for tonight,"

She glances down, taking in the mounds of chaos around me. I can tell that she thinks I'm being ridiculous.

"Mom!" I whine. "Tonight is a huge deal for me, and all my

clothes are too tight and too short. Everything I own is slutty. Can you please take me shopping?"

Relief passes over her face as she stares down at me. "I thought you would never ask."

"Sweet, thanks. But what is that supposed to mean?"

"Honey," she laughs, "I've been praying for the day that you would finally come to your senses and put on some clothes. I love you no matter what, but sometimes, it's embarrassing to be seen in public with you."

I'm not sure how I feel about that statement, but this probably isn't the time to get defensive. Besides, when I think about some of the things I've worn in public, I'm embarrassed for myself too.

"Get ready, and let's go shopping. But we aren't going to be buying a lot of stuff. We leave for Kentucky in a month and need to be saving money for that."

Jumping up, I throw my arms around her. "Thanks, Mom."

We spend the better part of the afternoon shopping, laughing, and rebuilding our bond. Mother-daughter time is far different now that I'm clean, and it becomes even more evident as the day goes on.

She looks surprised when I ask her to come into the fitting room with me. For years, I refused to let her see me naked because of the track marks that covered my body. She looks apprehensive when I ask for her honest opinion on the clothes I've picked. I used to scream at her when she said something I didn't want to hear. Now, she looks relieved when I don't.

She takes me out to lunch and smiles as she watches me actually eat the food I ordered. We both get ice cream for dessert and walk around the mall, just enjoying our time together. I'm not in a rush to go chase dope, and I don't disappear into random bathrooms to shoot up while she waits for me outside. I catch my mom looking at me—hope and faith written all over her beautiful face—and I know that nobody in the world will ever love me the way she does. The moment hits me, and I stop, grab her shoulder, and turn her to face me.

"Mom, I'm so sorry, I—"

"No," she interrupts, "you don't have to apologize anymore. I forgive you for everything you have ever done. You are my daughter, and there is nothing you could ever do that would be unforgivable to me."

Standing there with tears rolling down both of our faces, I realize how much I needed her to say those words.

"We need to stop," she whispers, pulling me into a hug, "because now you look ugly, and I have to go poop." We laugh through our tears.

Love, forgiveness, laughter, tears, and shopping—the cornerstone of mothers and daughters—was in our blood.

Sitting in my car, I curse the rain that has been steadily falling since I parked. It's annoying that after such a great day with my mom and the hours of effort it took to look my best, nature was going to screw it all up. The wet drizzle wouldn't have been a problem if I had just listened to my mom when she told me to take an umbrella. You should always listen to your mother.

I glance up at the windshield and watch as fat drops of water burst against the glass. I check the clock on the dash; I'm going to have to hurry, or I'll be late to my own party.

I quickly scan the contents of my car, trying to find something to use for cover. I consider dumping the contents out of a McDonald's bag and using that, but the smell of onions changes my mind. Out of options, I'm just going to have to make a run for it and hope for the best.

I lift my hands to my head, swirl my hair around my finger and tie it in a knot at the base of my skull. Taking a deep breath, I grab the door handle and slip out of the car in one motion. Choosing my steps carefully so that I don't fall on the uneven pavement and bust my ass, I cross the parking lot and hurry toward the old building. Drops of rain land on my neck and trickle down my back. I rush the last ten yards to the side of the building where the roof's eave offers cover.

I take a second to release my hair, then reach down and smooth out the black pencil skirt I got today. It goes perfectly with the emerald blouse my mom had chosen. We were both shocked when I decided to rock it tonight. I was probably ten years old the last time I had willingly worn anything she picked out.

I walk along the wall and turn the corner that leads to the entrance. With a final glance down my body to make sure a boob wasn't hanging out or that I didn't have a piece of trash stuck to my shoe, I pull open the doors and step directly into a silent room full of people. I watch as heads turn in my direction, nearly giving me an anxiety attack—and I don't even have anxiety.

To escape the sudden pressure that hits me, I avert my eyes and hurry toward the back of the room. My black stilettos echo on the white tiles as I spot an empty seat and lower myself into it. I cross my legs and pray that my cellulite isn't showing, then direct my attention to the front of the room.

I guess I'm not as late as I thought; the meeting hasn't even started. I watch as some dude sets out cups and starts a pot of coffee, and the unmistakable scent reaches my nose pretty fast—the same smell that gets me out of bed in the morning. I'm thinking about grabbing a cup when I hear a question that makes me freeze in place.

"Hey, do you want to read the traditions?"

Oh, God, I hope they aren't talking to me. There was no way in hell that I would read anything during a meeting, and it most surely wouldn't be "The Traditions" if I did.

I've had some pretty humiliating moments in my life—I mean, really cringy shit—but nothing compares to the moment I disgraced myself over the pronunciation of a single word. One. Stupid. Word. And I was cut off at the knees.

I had been at a meeting in Austin, Texas, fresh off meth and feeling better than I had in years. There were at least a hundred people in the room, and when they asked for volunteers to read the literature, I raised my hand. I'm an educated woman with a solid command of the English language, so I was pretty confident that I could handle a single sheet of numerically listed statements.

I was breezing right through until I got to number eleven. My eyes were a fraction of a second ahead of my mouth, and when they passed over a specific word, I frantically tried to sound it out in my head before my mouth caught up. But I was too late.

"Anon-e-mtee." *Oh, shit.* "An-eee-mty."

After the second mispronunciation, I stopped and took a second to try and work it out under my breath. I could feel the crushing weight of a hundred eyes drill into me, and I wanted to die.

"AAAAnnn-ee-miDDy"

Oh. My. God.

It was just getting worse. I wasn't sure what to do at that point, so I stared down at the paper intently, willing the word to change from "anonymity" into something that I could pronounce. Looking up, I silently begged for somebody—anybody—to step in and stop this madness, but nobody did. I looked back down and knew that there would be no coming back from this, no matter what I said next. So, I grabbed my purse off the floor and walked out, leaving "The Traditions" floating in my wake.

Anonymity. Stupid freaking word; Webster needs to remove it from the dictionary.

That voice once again knocks me off of memory lane. "Excuse me, but do you want to read?" I look up and see an older guy with thin lips and a round face peering at me over wire-rimmed glasses.

"No, but thank you," I say politely.

He stares at me for a long second, his face twisting into a scowl, before turning around and dismissing me. He passes the page off to the lady next to him without a word. I bet he doesn't know how to pronounce it either.

The room quiets when the meeting begins a few minutes later. I listen as the literature is read and hold my breath when the lady recites "The Traditions" and enunciates the dreaded word correctly. I shoot daggers of envy into the back of her head, then tune out the rest.

I know that all of this is important. I really do. But I'm having a hard time focusing on anything except the end of the meeting. Pulling out my phone, I check the time and almost sigh out loud. Barely ten minutes have passed since I walked in the door.

I direct my attention back to the chick that's sharing, and my heart catches when she tells the group that she lost her children while in active addiction. Today, she found out that her rights had been terminated, and she has no hope of ever getting them back. I can hear the tears in her voice, and I just want to wrap her up in my arms and tell her that it will be okay. But will it? She will have to live the rest of her life knowing that she will never see her children again, and I can't imagine that ever being okay.

I listen as she breaks down, and I want to cry with her. Damn, I don't think I would be able to stay clean if I lost Mason forever. What would be the point? I can't envision a world where I'm not his mom. I have picked drugs over him for the last four years, but I always knew that I would find my way back to him one day. After listening to the girl share, I'm sure that she probably thought the same thing. And then, one day, she woke up and the chance was lost.

She doubles over into herself, and the magnitude of her situation resonates through the room. She lifts her arm and waves her hand, indicating that we should continue; she is done sharing. I feel sick for this young girl, but I can't help but feel a tremendous amount of gratitude that I still have a chance to be in Mason's life. I also feel guilty because I'm still excited about what happens at the end of the meeting, despite the anguish that was just shared. The next thirty minutes drag on slowly, but finally, there is nobody left to share, and the announcements have been read.

I keep my face blank as I glance around the room. I try not to fidget, but it seems like the tweak in me is still strong. Plus, my ass is falling asleep. I don't want anybody to think that I care, but inside, I'm shaking with anticipation.

"This group recognizes the length of clean time by handing out key tags. If you have one coming to you, please come up and get it. And a hug," adds Kristen, her voice flat.

Inwardly, I roll my eyes and sigh. Why does it have to be Kristen handing out key tags tonight? Out of all the people in the room, on my big night, the only chick in these meetings I cannot stand will be the one handing me my award.

It's almost like she is doing this on purpose to ruin my night. She hasn't liked me from the first moment I had walked into this room. She never returns a smile and always seems to be judging everything I say or do. She always signs up to chair the meetings and proceeds to lord over the group, talking down to us like she knows everything. Suffice to say; she gets on my nerves.

"The white key tag is the international color of surrender," Kristen says, without emotion. "This key tag is for anyone back after a relapse, at their first meeting, or just want to surrender to their disease today. Does anyone want to give up their old ways for a new way?"

A few people make their way up to collect a tag, and I wonder if they had relapsed or if this was their first time here. I've heard about people that compile the white key tags like candy because they keep relapsing. At least they keep trying, I suppose, but I hope I never turn into one of those people.

As they return to their seats, Kristen moves on, picking up an orange key tag. "Anybody with thirty days can come up and grab their orange key tag. Orange is the color of caution, reminding us that we should be cautious at thirty days. Avoid old playmates, playgrounds, and playthings."

As a new group of people wandered up to the front, I remember how relieved I was when I hit thirty days. It had been the most challenging month of my entire life, and I never wanted to have to go through that shit again.

I watch as they smile, trade hugs, and grab the pieces of cheap plastic. To ordinary people, the innocuous teardrop-shaped keyring is just a way to organize their keys. But for us, it means that we stopped killing ourselves thirty days ago.

"Anybody got sixty days clean and serene? The color of a FROG reminding us to Fully Rely On God."

This is it, the moment I have been waiting for all day. Practically jumping out of my chair, I toss my hair back over my shoulder and walk to the front of the room like I'm accepting an

Academy Award. The air surrounding me feels heavy, and the buzzing in my ears drowns out the sound of clapping.

When I get to the front of the room, I reach my hand out, grab my green tag, and hold it over my heart. The moment overcomes me, and I plaster a massive smile on my face, letting Kristen pull me into a hug. As her arms circle my waist, she leans in closer and whispers in my ear, "I am so proud of you."

In total shock, I pull away and stare, searching her face for clues that she might be screwing with me. But she is smiling, and it looks genuine. I reach back towards her and hug her tight, swamped with gratitude. As I step away and turn around, I look out into the room to see everybody smiling back at me. They know what it took to get here, and feeling their love and acceptance makes my eyes blur.

I walk back to my seat and slide quickly into the chair. Glancing down, I flip the key chain over in my hand and run my fingers across the front. I honestly have no idea how I made it this far, but I know that I wouldn't have even begun if not for God.

I haven't touched meth or a needle for sixty consecutive days. Not even once. I remember when I couldn't put together sixty minutes, let alone sixty days. If I wasn't getting high, I was thinking about getting high or worried about getting more dope so that I could get high. That had been my entire life for years, and it feels surreal that it no longer is.

I feel a real sense of pride and accomplishment. Every single day, I have moments when I want to give up, but I've stuck it out. Sometimes it's been second by second, but I've done it.

Lost in my thoughts, I miss the rest of the meeting. Suddenly, everybody is standing and gathering into a circle around the room. I slip between two women I had never seen before and reach for their hands. We smile at each other, and I know that I am exactly where I am supposed to be.

Bowing our heads, we close the meeting with the serenity prayer, and the power of our voices moving together in unity touches my soul.

"God, grant me the serenity to accept the things I cannot change, the courage to change the things I can, and the wisdom to know the difference."

I haven't felt very serene the last two months, and I know that I tend to mistake wisdom for self-will, but I feel pretty confident about the courage part of the prayer. I have sixty days clean, after all.

With the meeting over, we all make our way outside. Besides collecting my hard-won key tags, this was usually my favorite part of these meetings; the social element, where we would stand around, smoke, and talk. I have met some great people since I got home, and I feel like I've been making friends with the right kind of people.

I've heard people say that if you want to find drugs, hit a twelve-step meeting. But that just hasn't ever been my experience. Never once has anybody offered me dope or alluded to getting high. I guess that if I had been looking for it, I could find it. That is why I am so damn scared to leave my mom's house most of the time and how I know I can't be around people that are getting high. One moment of weakness or a lapse in judgment, and I would have to start this whole thing over again. Then, I would have to pick up a second white key tag, and that just isn't going to work for me.

I glance around at this group of misfits; these are my people. The broken trying to heal. It's almost like they understand me, even when I say nothing. Our stories all may be different, but we have all been on the same journey together.

While I would typically hang out here until everybody was gone, tonight, I just want to get home. I can't wait to show my mom the little green beauty that I stuck in my wallet. She will be thrilled, and it makes me happy to think that finally, after years of heartbreak and disappointment, I am giving her a reason to be proud of me again.

Every day that passes, I see the hope grow behind her eyes. At first, she was very cautious and uncertain, scared to believe that maybe I would succeed where my brother had failed. She doesn't want to lose another child, and she is doing everything she can to make sure that I don't die. I'm going to do everything I can to make sure that doesn't happen either.

I try to tell her not to worry, but she's a mom; they worry no matter what. I know that she studies me for signs that I have relapsed, and I keep assuring her that she would know. "Mom, if I start vacuuming the drive-way or stop eating, those will be clear indications that I've fallen off the wagon," I'll sometimes laugh. "You will know, I promise."

The other night, while we were sitting on her back porch, she began to cry out of the blue.

"Mom, what is wrong with you?" I asked, alarmed.

She looked at me and said, "I'm just grateful to God that I have my daughter back."

If I'm not going to stay clean for myself, I will stay clean for her. I'm going to do the right things and make the right choices. I have to; this is my only chance to fight my way back to the life I had before dope. I want that life back more than anything. I want to be financially stable, professionally successful, and a present mom and daughter. And I want Cage and me to get married, stay clean, and have a baby or two. I want my whole-ass old life back.

I say my goodbyes and walk back to my car. The storm had passed, and now the sky is clear; dozens of stars twinkle above my head. As I open my car door, I glance up and smile. I feel like everything will be okay, and it's been a very long time since I've felt that way.

A sudden desire to talk to Cage, to celebrate this night with him, overwhelms me. I wish I were going home to him. I imagine walking into his arms and feeling him pick me up as I wrap my legs around his waist, feeling safe and loved. I ache for that right now.

I miss hearing him call me Wind. Even in his letter, he hadn't addressed it to "Wind," writing my first name instead. It's a slap in the face for him to call me by my real name; he only used it when he hated me. And it seems like he has been calling me Amanda ever since he went to jail and I continued to get high.

Calling me Wind was reserved for the times he loved me, and everything was right in our world. It's been a million lifetimes since anything was right, but the last sixty days feel like a good start.

It's driving me crazy that he hasn't seen me since I got clean. I feel like if he would just see me, we could fix all the damage we had caused to our relationship and start over. If he could look into my eyes, he would know that I was telling the truth about being clean. If he could hear my voice and see my face when I tell him how sorry I am, then maybe he could start to forgive me.

It feels so much longer than four years ago that we met and fell in love, and I wonder if he thinks about that time at all; the life we had together. It was like magic from the very first moment. We never spent a day apart, and our love set the world on fire. We danced every night, rocked out at every concert we could find, and our sex was the best I can imagine sex being. We were happy. I know that we were. It was the kind of love that should have lasted forever, but then heroin and meth came calling and ripped it all apart. He ended up in jail, and I ended up spending years on the street, feeding my habit and trying to forget.

I don't want to forget anymore. I want my life back, and that includes Cage. He needs to get on board with this because there is no other way our story can end. There is no other option in my mind except getting back together.

I pull out my phone and decide to write to him.

Dear Cage,

After your last letter, I promised myself that I would never write to you again. I swore to myself that I would just move on and forget you. I wish it were that easy, but we both know that it's not. We're connected, Cage and Wind forever, remember?

Today has been a big day for me, and you are the only person in the world I want to share it with. Today, I celebrated 60 days clean! I just picked up my green key tag, green like your eyes. Okay, not the same green as your eyes, but it still reminds me of you.

I know that I have given you years of reasons not to believe me, but I swear to

God on everything I love, or will ever love, that I am telling the truth! I haven't gotten high once. I rarely leave my mom's house unless I'm with her or going to a meeting.

I'm scared, Cage. Staying clean is so hard. I know I don't have any right to ask you this, but I think seeing you would help. I have nobody to talk to that knows me the way you do. I scare my mom when I talk about how hard this is; she just panics and takes my car keys away. And I want to see you because for the first time in years, we're both clean.

Also, I need to see you because I have to tell you something. I'm trying to do the right thing, and getting Mason back is the most right thing I can imagine doing. So, I'm leaving Texas and heading to Kentucky soon, and I need you to tell me that it's ok to go. I can't leave until I hear you tell me that I'm doing the right thing.

I hope that the Wind still reminds you of me.

4

THE CALL

I drop the shovel full of gravel into the wheelbarrow, and my body aches in protest. The afternoon sun beats on my neck as sweat drip down my chest, running like a river between my tits. My mom walks towards me. She looks as filthy and worn out as me but still has a smile on her beautiful face as she passes me a bottle of cold water.

"What are you smiling at?" I ask as I take a swig.

"You just look so cute doing that."

"Bullshit! I'm covered in dirt, and I'm pouring sweat." Rolling my eyes at her, I squirt the water onto my face and feel it splash down my chest.

"I know, but I love that we are doing this together. And we're almost done."

My mom wanted her backyard landscaped professionally but realized that she couldn't afford it after getting multiple quotes. She was so disappointed, and I knew that the reason she didn't have the money was that she had spent so much for me to go to rehab, and now she was paying for me to move to Kentucky. I felt terrible and suggested that maybe we could figure out how to do some of the things she wanted ourselves. I mean, how hard could it be to build a stone walkway, a few raised flower beds, and install a dry creek bed with a French drain?

It turns out, pretty damn difficult. Moving tons of gravel from the driveway into the backyard, one wheelbarrow at a time, takes a long time and requires a lot of energy. And it's exhausting. More than once, my brain has tried to trick me into believing that a shot of meth was the answer to my problems. And then I remind myself that the reality of making that decision would result in a project that was never finished because I had sold the gravel at a quarter of its cost to buy more dope and trying to convince my mom that the rocks had all blown away in some freak storm.

I look at my mom and study her face. I can see how happy she is over something as simple as doing yard work with her daughter, and it moves me. My addiction had been her living nightmare; she had walked into hell, stood beside me, and burned with me. I honestly can't even imagine the agony she had been through over the last four years. My pain was her pain, except I was too numb to feel anything, whereas she had felt everything—every tear, every terrifying moment, and every agonizing scream. She never left and never stopped fighting or praying that I would come back to her one day.

And here I am, still broken in places, but healing a little more every day. I know the road in front of me will be difficult and the challenges many, but my mom will be there, battling right beside me. There is nothing on earth more powerful than the love of a mother. And I have a badass mom.

We watch Tempest as her body becomes still, and the fur rises across the top of her back, her eyes on a squirrel. Doberman ears standing strong and proud, she slowly moves forward, painstakingly lifting one leg after the other in total silence. She pauses between each step, stalking her prey like a predator in the wild.

As she moves closer to the squirrel, I hold my breath, worried that this will be the time she catches it. This same scene has played out at least a hundred times before, and Tempest has never been successful. I don't want her to be; I love our yard squirrels and would be devastated if anything happened to them.

I'm about to call out and warn the squirrel to run when she notices Tempest and makes a break towards the back fence, bolting as fast as her little legs will carry her. Silently, I cheer her on as Tempest barks and follows in pursuit. The squirrel leaps onto the fence and scrambles to the top, while my dog crashes into the wood slats with a loud thump.

Tempest stares in defeat at the squirrel peering down at her, gleeful in victory. I stand there, smiling like an idiot, and realize how much I love my new life. I'm spending time with my mom, watching my dog spaz out, and I don't have a monkey on my back anymore.

"This is the last of it," I say as I dump the rocks into the corner of the yard, watching as they tumble and spread out at my feet.

"All we need to do is install the flower box beneath the window, and we'll be done."

My brow furrows. "Mom, are you sure you know what you're doing? Drilling into a brick wall seems like some advanced construction shit."

"Of course!" Sounding far more confident than I think she should be, she walks towards the side of the wall and kneels beneath the window.

My gaze sweeps across the backyard, and I think about what a trip my mom is. Metal signs and brightly colored decorations are installed on the fence that runs across the back of her entire property. Purple and blue tin butterflies and bright orange lanterns hang from the pickets. Shiny pink and green steel flowers dangle from the ledge's top, and squirrel feeders are attached to every post. It looks like we went down the rabbit hole into Wonderland, but my mom loves it, and that's all that matters.

I turn back to the house just as my mom presses the drill into the wall. The loud whining sound as it turns makes my skin crawl. Suddenly, brick dust and large pieces of debris start flying everywhere. I quickly step towards her and touch her on the back of the shoulder to get her attention.

"Mom, this is dangerous. We need safety glasses."

"Just close your eyes, stupid."

My jaw drops. "Oh, my God, mom, have you lost your mind? What is wrong with you?" Suddenly, I feel like the parent. "I'm going to run down to the hardware store and get glasses, do not proceed until I get home."

She lets out an exasperated sigh and rolls her eyes. "Fine."

"Look, woman, if you don't stop acting crazy, I'm going to put you into an old folks home," I snicker. "Next thing I know, you're going to be walking down the street in your bathrobe."

"Just shut up. I'm not going to wait all day, so you better hurry."

My mom is wild, I think, as I head inside to grab my keys. Just as I'm closing the back door, my phone rings. I don't recognize the number and consider letting it go to voicemail because I'm sure it's just a creditor calling to ask for money that I don't have. Ultimately, I decide to answer; I can just hang up if it's the vultures calling.

"Hello?" I say impatiently.

There is a short click, and a robotic voice announces that I am receiving a call from an inmate at the Texas Department of Corrections. My breath catches as the words set off a ringing in my ears. Time stops as I lean back against the door and feel myself slide slowly to the floor. My ass hits the cold tile, and his name slips out of my mouth in a whisper.

Cage.

I haven't heard his voice in months, and the significance of this call slams into me. My phone feels like it weighs a million pounds, and I have a sudden urge to disconnect the call. I wasn't ready; I needed time to get my thoughts in order before I spoke to him.

My mind goes to war with itself, and questions flood my brain. What if he doesn't call me back? What if this is my only chance to speak to him? What if he is calling me to forgive me and tell me he loves me? My mind is racing, and I only have seconds to collect myself. Taking a deep breath, I pull myself together. This was Cage we're talking about; of course I'm going to take his call.

I try to focus on the mechanical voice as it leads me through the available options, but I'm so freaked out that I miss the number that I'm supposed to hit to accept the call. Was it three or four? *Shit.*

"Please press five to block this caller," the emotionless voice says.

I watch my thumb tremble as it moves across the screen. Hesitating for a second, I finally click on the number three, hoping that it's the right digit. After a moment of silence that feels like a thousand seconds, I hear it. The name that can jumpstart my soul and said by the man that had changed my life.

"Wind."

His voice travels into my ear and lands in the center of my

Addict Chick unCaged

chest. My heart starts to swing between my ribs as his sexy face flashes into my mind—piercing green eyes that could stare straight into my soul, a jawline that was as sharp as granite, and a mouth that had kissed every inch of my body.

The relief is instant. He called me Wind, not Amanda. Clearly, my last letter had smoothed things over, and everything was going to be okay.

The silence stretches between us, and I struggle to say something so that he doesn't hang up. Sounding like a teenage girl, the best I can manage is, "Hi!"

"Baby, it's so good to hear your voice!" I can hear the smile in his tone, and it sounds like he means it.

"I'm so glad you called; I have been missing you like crazy." If he only knew how much. "I wasn't sure if I would ever hear from you again after the letter I sent you."

"You wouldn't have, but then I got the other one and wanted to tell you something."

Before he can tell me what that was, I interrupt. "I'm sorry for what I said. I really am. I was upset, and you hurt me with that drawing."

Cage doesn't acknowledge my apologies or extend a branch of forgiveness. He just responds with, "I called to tell you that I'm glad you're leaving, and I think you should."

I'm confused by his statement, unsure if he is trying to be encouraging or just a complete asshole. I decide that it's better for my mental health if I assume that he is being supportive.

"Guess what?" I ask.

"What?"

"I'll have ninety days clean in a few days!" I expect him to congratulate me and say that he's proud of me; I'm finally doing what he told me to do years ago, and I needed his approval. I would be getting none of that.

"Yeah?" His voice is full of doubt.

My response matches his. "Yeah."

He doesn't believe me. I probably shouldn't be surprised. I have told him I was clean a million times before. Every time I ever spoke to him, I swore that I wasn't getting high anymore. I'd written him at least a hundred letters to share the news that I was three, twenty, ninety days clean, all lies.

I remember how hard I had to work to keep the days straight in my head to match up with the dates of the letters. God only knows how inaccurate it all had been. He knew, of course. Cage knew me better than I knew myself. But he would pretend to believe me, and maybe he even lied to himself.

Not wanting this conversation to go sideways, I say, "I'm leaving for Kentucky in a week and would love to see you before I go; please put me on your visitors' list."

His reply is hard, fast, and final. "No."

I can't hide my shock. "Cage, please! I want to see you before I go. I need to see you before I leave." I can hear the desperation in my voice and know that I sound pathetic, but I don't care. "I can't leave until you see I'm clean."

How is this even happening right now? In what world am I living in that Cage wouldn't want to see me? I press my back against the door and feel my anxiety start to grow like a burning fire inside my gut, shooting through my body one inch at a time.

"Please don't do this to me," I wail, my hysteria rising.

"Wind, shut the fuck up and listen," Cage barks, and I instantly shut my mouth as though I had just been slapped. He is the only person in the world that can talk to me like that and have me listen. If anybody else had said that to me, I would have done the complete opposite of shutting the fuck up.

After a long pause, Cage's voice reaches across the miles and delivers the killing blow. "Do I hope that you're clean? Of course, I do!" His voice is heavy with emotion and an accusation that I don't want to hear. "But do you remember the last time you told me that you were clean? When you swore up and down that you had been clean? That you had gotten your shit together and were building a life for us? You lied then. I wanted it to be true so badly! I trusted you, and you lied!"

Here it is, the moment I knew that one day I was going to have to face. The crossroads in which I have to stop blaming Cage for what our love had become and start owning my part in the destruction.

"Do you think I will ever forgive you for what you did?" he rages on, and the hate I hear in his voice is as powerful as the hostility I feel for myself.

The disgust of knowing that we are here because of what I did is more than I can handle. My lower lip quivers, and I start to cry, the tears spilling down my face unchecked. I don't resist as my body shakes with sobs. Cage is right. What I did to him was far worse than anything he ever did to me. Did I think he would just forget or absolve me of my sins? I prayed that he would, but deep down, I always knew that wouldn't.

He won't forgive me because what I did was unforgivable.

But like a dog backed into a corner, my defenses rise, and I respond with equal amounts of hate, the bitterness thick in my voice. "Forgiveness? Don't you think you should be begging for mine too? We both screwed up, and neither of us deserves forgiveness. We're even now, Cage, don't you think?"

Are we even though? If we were keeping score of who had hurt the other worse, wouldn't I be winning? What I did to him was intentional, vicious, and sickening.

We all have a story to tell and secrets to hide, what I did to Cage—when I was still getting high and in active addiction—is mine. It wouldn't be fair if I left this part out.

5

ACTIVE ADDICTION

"Cage, I swear, I've been clean for over three months now," I lie, my voice full of frustration. "I told you that I was going to get my shit together, and I have!" Wishing I had never answered this call, I stare up at the ceiling fan in my bedroom and consider flinging my phone right into the blades.

"Baby, I just wanted to check on you and make sure. I'm proud of you and can't wait until you're picking me up in a few days. I'm ready to get the hell out of here and home to my woman!" I can hear the truth and excitement in his voice.

I feel the weight of my lie roll through me and know that time is running out. The anxiety makes my resentment for Cage grow. He thinks it's easy to get clean, but the only times he's ever gotten clean were when he went to jail. If I were locked up with zero chances of getting high, I would be clean too. It's much more difficult when you can find dope right down the street.

Forcing a smile onto my face, I say, "I will be there waiting for you the minute you walk out those doors!" My brain is racing at a million miles an hour, thoughts and feelings tumbling together.

"How is the new job going? Have you saved any money?" His questions come fast, and I struggle for an answer that will sound like the truth.

"It's good! A slow start, but I've done a couple of jobs designing business cards and shit. The way the accounting works, I won't get paid on any of it for a month," I say, hoping that I can actually get a few jobs before the month is over. "I just started, so it might take a while before I get more projects to work on, but you have to start somewhere, right?" I give a fake laugh, trying to sound upbeat.

Apprehension fills me when I realize how badly I'm screwing up. I told Cage that I started working for an online platform that hires freelancers and contractors for design work and digital marketing projects. It wasn't a total lie; I *had* created an account; I just haven't filled out my profile yet. Or bid on any projects so that I can start earning money. I have no idea why I haven't done it yet, except that something always seems to come up. As soon as Cage and I hang up, I'll get it taken care of.

"The first thing I'm doing is getting a job. I want to get a place of our own as quickly as possible," Cage says, breaking into my thoughts.

Laughing, I say, "That's the first thing you're going to do, huh?"

His response is perfect. "Wind, the first thing I am going to do is take you to bed, make love to every inch of your body, and then I am going to bang your wicked brains out."

Instantly, I am wet—soaking wet—and I pulse between my legs. All thoughts of getting a job, my numerous lies, and the multitude of sins flee, and the only thing I can think about is Cage and setting the world on fire with our bodies.

Before I can respond, Cage douses the heat beating through

my body with his icy words, delivered like a dagger straight across the miles separating us and right into my black heart. "Wind, you better not be lying to me."

Oh, God, he knows! Panic surges through me like a torrent from hell, and I feel like a cat without whiskers fumbling around in the dark, searching for the right response to his statement. Maybe I should just be honest with him and tell him what I'm pretty sure he already knows— that I'm a failure and a liar.

Reaching inside myself, I attempt to harness the love we once had. I know that the woman I used to be would tell him the truth; that woman never lied to Cage—not ever. And that chick had loved Cage so much that she would be honest right now because she would do anything to keep him safe, even if it meant keeping him safe from herself.

But telling him the truth would destroy everything. Our future together would be lost forever, our second chance at life gone before it had even begun. I did not doubt that if Cage knew the truth, he would leave me here, stuck in the dope game, and dying a little more every single day while he went on with his life as if I had never existed. I want to scream at him that it's not freaking fair.

As the silence grows, the pressure inside my head explodes, and I do the only thing I know how to do. I lie.

"Cage, I'm not lying, but I am getting sick of your accusations! Every time you call me, you pull this shit!" I can hear the rage in my voice, and I don't even try to control it. "Look, I have to get back to work, and I don't have time for this right now. I'm hanging up, and you can call me back when you decide to trust me. If I don't hear from you, I will see you in a few days. I love you." Anxious to cut this off before he backed me into another corner, I end the call.

I chew my lip, worried that I've just made a colossal mistake.

Cage is going to be pissed that I dared to hang up on him. Even worse, I was going to have to get clean for me to fix this mess.

Regret washes through me in terrifying waves. Our last chance together is slipping away, and the only thing I have to do to save it is to stop picking up dope. That's it. Just stop getting high. With everything that was on the line, it should be so easy, but it's not.

Since the day Cage had called to tell me that he would be getting out in a few months, I had tried to get clean. I had tried *so* hard to do what he had told me to do—what he needed me to do—so that we could be together. Sometimes I could make it the entire day without shooting up, but eventually, the demon would swoop inside my head, and I would be screaming for relief.

Back and forth, the war wage inside my head. I forever felt like I needed dope to get even be able to get clean. So, I would get a little stash and separate into smaller shots, just to get through the day. Inevitably, as soon as I had done my last shot, I needed more so that I could start again. It felt like groundhog's day, every day. The days began to blur, and despite my best efforts, I couldn't stop getting high.

My entire world exists on a merry-go-round from hell that never stops. I'm standing on a slick platform, surrounded by eerie horses frozen in mid-gallop. Getting high is like climbing into the jeweled saddle of the wooden stallion and wrapping my hands around the pole that connects it to the floor. As the ride begins to rotate, the mechanical music builds, drowning out any thought other than the dope coursing through my blood. The ground disappears beneath me, and I climb higher.

Throwing my head back, I stare up at the flashing white bulbs that hang across the ceiling, the points of light becoming smaller as my horse slowly lowers. It's time to get off, so I slide down the side of the beast and walk toward my new life without the use of drugs.

As I near the edge, getting ready to jump off the merry-go-round, I stop and stare into the night. It starts spinning faster and faster and the desperation to get away rises inside me, but I cannot even garner the courage to throw myself off, even if that is the only way to save my life. Catching sight of myself in a gilded mirror, my mouth forms words and sends them back to me.

Just. One. More.

And I turn, walk back to that same horse, climb onto his back, and let him take me back up to ride the crest all over again.

I'm running out of time, and as Cage's release date races toward me, my lies begin to pile up, crushing me. I most certainly do not have my shit together. 'Together' is the very last thing in the world that my shit is. Not even close.

Looking down at my phone, I will it to ring. I want Cage to call me back. I want to tell him the truth; I can't take it anymore. I want to beg him to save me, but mostly I want him to hate me and release me from this impossible obligation. I want to tell him to find somebody else because I'm not strong enough. My mind spins, and I feel like I'm being torn into a million tiny pieces.

The words he said to me all those years ago echo in my mind. "Wind, you have tried everything else to save me, and you are the strongest woman I have ever met. If you let me shoot you up, you will understand and be strong enough to bring us both back." And like so many times before, I think back to that moment and try and figure out what his true motivations had been that day. Had he really believed that I was going to be strong enough to save us both? Or were his words born from a place of utter selfishness?

In the dark place of my brain where the meth demon lives, Lucifer breathes whispers that flood my head with the answer that

I already know—that I probably always have known, even before I let Cage shoot me up for the first time. The answer Cage knew before he slid a needle into my arm and destroyed both of our lives. He knew exactly what would happen to me. My strength of will was nothing compared to the feeling of meth. And he shot me up anyway because he didn't want to be alone. He wanted me with him, even if it meant destroying my life right beside his.

As the seconds stretch into long minutes and the phone doesn't ring, I feel resentment start to boil inside me. Cage isn't going to call because he expects me to do whatever he wants. I think back to the calls and letters full of condemnation in which he expected me to do what he had never been able to do on his own. He demanded that I do for him what he had been unwilling to do for me. Get clean, get my shit together, and build a new life so that he could get out of jail and just slip right back into my life with me having done all the hard work by myself.

Fuck him.

Tossing my phone on the bed, go to my bathroom and reach under the sink. I feel for the makeup bag I have taped behind to the top of the false drawer and pull it out, staring inside. My dope kit has five rigs left and enough for maybe three small shots. But I don't want a little shot right now; I want to blast myself into feeling better, knowing that that is where I will find the answers I'm seeking.

I make a shot and sit right down on the bathroom floor. I look for the nick on my wrist, the evidence of a good vein, and slip the needle in without ceremony.

My eyes close, and I lean back against the wall, letting the dope take me. As the heat spreads through me and my breath catches in a shallow cough, I free fall into the darkness. And in the deepest part of my soul, a sickness grows. I gravitate towards it, feeling it bury me in hate.

I'm going to match Cage, word for word, and see if he's strong enough to follow me into hell and bring us both back. *It's only fair,* I muse. I'm going to give him the same chance he had given me—a last-ditch effort to save us both. I know he will fail, though. Cage has never been stronger than me, even on his very best day.

I watch in satisfaction as a bead of blood rolls down my hand and drops to the floor.

The heat from the pavement radiates toward me in waves as I walk across the parking lot. A thin layer of perspiration forms on my arms, and I worry that I'm about to sweat off the body makeup I had just applied over the bruises and track marks.

Two flagpoles guard the entrance to the county jail, the United States flag and the Texas flag. Despite a small breeze pushing the hot air around, the flags lay limply against the poles, like a dick that won't get hard. I make a beeline toward the jail entrance, anxious to get out of the heat. A rush of cold air greets me as I push the doors open. The extreme temperature change is almost painful, but at least the sweat on my neck has stopped dripping between my boobs.

Surveying the lobby, I search for the information desk. It's on the far side of the room, and I quickly make my way to the counter. The man behind the thick plexiglass is playing on his phone, and the only thing I can see is the polished top of his bald head. I shift my body, trying to get his attention, but he doesn't move. Sighing loudly, I impatiently wait for him to acknowledge me.

After a few minutes, I tap on the glass with my fingernails and say, "Excuse me?"

The dickhead cop finally tilts his head back and looks at me.

I take in his square-shaped face, ruddy complexion, and bushy eyebrows. His eyes are pale blue, almost translucent, and they squint at me through his thin wire-framed glasses; he had a face that was boring and uninteresting. He looked like the kind of man that would get out of the shower to take a piss. The silver nameplate attached to his uniform read, "M. Norman," and I instantly think of Norman Bates from *Psycho*, deciding that this dude lives with his mother.

"Yes?" he says, his tone arrogant.

Plastering a smile onto my face, I lean down and let my hair fall across my shoulders. I watch as his eyes follow the line of my collar bone and fall to my cleavage. Inwardly, I roll my eyes and think about how easy men are. "I'm picking up a prisoner that is being released today. Do you know what time that will be?"

His eyes never leave my chest. "No idea."

Irritated, I stand up and remove his line of sight. "Well, can you give me an idea?"

A long silence follows, and his ugly face peers back up at me, his mouth twisting into a scowl. "Sometime today." His tone proves that he is a man who relishes having control—the kind of power that comes with having a badge. He probably has a tiny dick and a wife that spanks his ass during sex.

"So, it could be in the next hour, or the next twelve hours, or what?" I ask, frustrated. The bastard doesn't say anything. He just stares back at me, his beady little eyes challenging me to say something else. "Lame," I whisper as I turn and walk away.

Heading back into the blistering heat, I trace the same route back to my mom's car and climb in. It feels like an oven, so I turn on the ignition and blast the air conditioner and sigh with relief when the cold air hits me in the face.

The day looms out in front of me, and I am not sure what I should do. It could be hours before Cage is released, and sitting here all day seems like a waste of time. I consider leaving to get high but quickly dismiss that thought. The jail is in the middle of nowhere, and I want to be here the second he walks out the doors. I have been fantasizing about this moment for months, and I'm not going to screw it up.

I reach into my bag and feel for my kit, needing to reassure myself that it hadn't grown legs, and walked away. For a second, I contemplate doing a shot right here in the jail parking lot; it would be hot to break the law right under their noses. And it would feel like a huge "fuck you" to that douche bag, Norman. But I had gotten high in a Starbucks bathroom a few hours ago and had spent a great deal of time painting over the proof of my deceit. The sick rainbow of fresh wounds and bruises would rat me out to Cage the second he sees them.

Besides, I've been getting high for days without any sleep, and I'm suddenly exhausted. My lids feel heavy, and I decide to rest my eyes for a few minutes. I click the lever to recline the top of the seat and close my eyes. Within seconds, my drained body pulls me into a deep sleep.

Hours must have passed, and I jerk awake as I feel a shadow cross my face. Eyes flying open, I launch myself forward and stare out the window, trying to figure out what the hell is going on. Oh, God, what time is it? How long have I been asleep? The sun has disappeared from the sky, and twilight has begun to spread across the parking lot, an orange glow barely lighting the sky.

"Fuck," I moan.

Panic rises when I realize that I have slept the entire day away. Where was Cage? Frantic, I glance out the window, willing my eyes to adjust to the dark. My eyes sweep the parking lot, searching for him. Just when I start to feel relief that I hadn't missed him, I spot somebody sitting on the curb. Bathed in shadows, the man is hunched over his knees, sitting completely still. It was Cage, and by the angle of his body, I knew he was furious. I have no idea how long he has been sitting there, waiting for me.

Damnit, I need a shot before I can deal with this. I look around for my bag but realize there is no way to do this here. I can't shoot up in the dark, and if I turn on the lights, he will see me for sure. I think about pulling out and driving down the road to hit, but it would be easier if I just got this over with first.

My eyes swivel back in his direction, and still, I don't move. Once upon a time, I would be jumping out and racing towards him like the blazes of hell were behind me. But now, I sit here and stare at him, annoyed that I can't get high because of him.

In the dark, I pull myself together as best as I can and pop a piece of gum into my mouth. Taking a deep breath, I open the door and swing my legs to the ground. I sweep a quick look down at my body and know that Cage will appreciate the way I look. Thanks to Sally Hansen's body makeup, I'm tan, and my skin looks smooth and perfect. I'm wearing the tightest shorts I own, and I'm skinnier than I have ever been. He is going to love my body even more once he gets me naked.

I ready my excuses for being late and take off walking towards the doors that I had exited from hours before. From the corner of my eye, I see him stand, rising through the shadows, and across the darkness, I hear him call my name. "Wind."

I turn around and feign surprise, a look of shock expertly plastered across my face. When I see Cage, free and rushing towards me, the outrage I felt towards him for standing in the way of my getting high disappears. Familiar memories flood my mind, and the connection between us pulls me forward. I take off running, not able to help myself.

Space closes between us, and just as he is reaching for me, my feet leave the ground, and I sail through the air, catapulting into his arms. Wrapping my legs tight around his waist, I feel his powerful arms pull me close, and our hearts slam into each other.

In this wild and beautiful moment, we are back to the couple we used to be, riding high on the excitement of falling in love and living for the seconds when we can be together. A time that we set the world on fire, and nothing could go wrong. I am being granted a few moments of everything we used to be, and I let it wash over me, feeling safe for the first time in a very long time.

"Cage! Oh my god, when did you get out? I've been waiting in my car all day and accidentally fell asleep!" My excuses pour out of me. "I am so sorry!"

"Baby, it doesn't even matter, you're here, and I am finally free!" I can feel the thrill of his words shoot through us both, and I pull back so that I can find his lips with my mouth.

Kissing him hungrily, I moan, "I love you so much."

He reaches up with one hand, pushes my head back, and bites my neck, branding me, marking me, owning me. Before I can even feel the pain, he is soothing it with his tongue and pulling my ear down to his mouth. "I love you too, Wind."

Reluctantly, hating for this moment to end, I slide down his body and stand before him, my face tilted up. He stares intently down at me and says, "Wind, I am so proud of you. You did it. We're finally both clean, and we can start over and move on with our lives."

I feel regret creep into my veins and freeze my blood.

Cage reaches down to grab the plastic garbage bag that holds all of his worldly possessions and turn so that I am standing beside him. He puts his arm around my shoulder and slides his hand to rest behind my neck. The movement feels so familiar; we used to walk everywhere like this, with him guiding and directing me to where he wanted us to go. I loved it because it made me feel protected and owned.

We walk toward my mom's car and load up all his shit. Cage tries to kiss me again, but I step away and say, "Let's get out of here!"

He seems surprised and takes a second to search my face. I'm trying so hard to keep myself in check, but inside, my brain screams for dope. I plant a quick kiss on his mouth and walk towards the driver seat and climb in,

As we are pulling out of the parking lot, Cage asks, "How long will it take to get to your mom's house?"

"Oh, babe, I have a surprise!" I respond excitedly. "I got us a hotel room in Dallas for the night!" Technically, my mom had paid for the accommodations, but since Cage thought I had a job, I didn't see any harm in letting him assume that I had.

I feel his head turn sharply towards me, and when I glance over, I see doubt spread across his face. His voice hard like steel, he says, "That's not a good idea. Dallas isn't good for either of us. We're heading straight to your mom's." He delivers this statement like a command. One that he expects me to follow.

Not this time, I think.

"Don't be silly. I can't wait that long to be on your dick, so we're headed to the hotel, and you're going to fuck me like you've been promising." I don't mention that he won't be banging me until after I get high.

He looks at me with surprise, shocked that I'm disobeying him. The silence that fills the car feels heavy, and I can feel him shooting glances at me. As we roll through the night, his silence starts to drown me. Feeling like the pressure will consume me, I lash out, "Why do you keep staring at me?"

His voice is low as he asks, "Wind, how long have you been clean now?"

Oh, shit. My brain moves in a million directions, and I try to scroll back to the last thing I had told him. Did I say that I had ninety days clean? More than that? Shit, was it less?

Sounding as defensive as I felt, I respond. "I don't know. I stopped keeping track."

"Take a guess, Wind."

"I honestly don't know! I stopped counting a few weeks ago because focusing on the number stressed me out. Maybe ninety-three or four?" It's a total shot in the dark.

Cage doesn't respond, and I don't know what to say. I know I should be feeling something right now, but all I can think about and is getting to the hotel so that I can get high. I know I can fix this, but I can't do it without a shot first. I'm so distracted that my car moves into the shoulder and begins to shake as we hit the rumble strips. I yank the car back into my lane and try to focus on my driving.

Suddenly the air in the car changes, and I can feel the instant he knows. Oh, God, he has figured it out. I was a fool to think that he wouldn't; Cage knows me better than anybody, and he had been an addict and lived in the dope game far longer than me. I risk a glance at him, and he stares back at me with horror and disbelief. The outrage on his face is real, and so is the hurt. I say nothing. I just return my gaze to the road and keep driving. Screw him and his judgments.

I keep expecting him to say something, to break the pressure that's building between us. I want him to yell and scream and call me a liar, but he stays silent. Anger would be easier to deal with than his silent condemnation. I shoot a glance at him from the corner of my eye. He is just looking out the window, stone-faced.

I nearly sigh with relief when I see the exit for our hotel ahead. I pull off and quickly turn into the parking lot. Slipping the car into park, I glance in the back seat at my overnight bag, wondering if I should take it. Maybe I can do a shot in the hotel lobby bathroom because I need to get well. I'm desperate to feel better. Cage is staring at me, so I quickly abandon the thought. Instead, I grab my wallet off the dash and say, "Babe, I'm going to get us checked in. I'll be right back."

Not waiting for his reply, I slip out of the car and head to the front desk, relieved to be away from him. I give the clerk my reservation number and wait for him to check me in. Fidgeting impatiently, I sign the paperwork, and five minutes later, I'm on my way back to the car with our room key.

Cage is standing outside of the car with my bag over his shoulder and the white trash bag at his feet. I can see the moon behind him, and somehow, it looks as dark as the night sky. The air is thick and heavy, and the effort it takes to walk across the parking lot covers me in sweat. Cage stares at me as I walk towards him, his face blank. For a second, our eyes find each other, and I can feel his pain echo across my heart. I avert my eyes, letting them fall to the ground.

Deciding that the fastest way to get to the room—and my kit—is to pretend that everything is fine, I smile. "We're in room 333, baby. Let's go." I slip my hand around his arm and lean into him, whispering excitedly, "I cannot wait to feel you inside me."

Cage remains quiet. I know I should be frightened by his

silence, but I keep reassuring myself that I can fix this. Everything is going to be okay. I have a plan, and it's going to be okay.

We ride the elevator up to the third floor and head to our room. Slipping the key into the lock, I open the door and walk inside. Glancing around, I see a king-size bed covered in a heavy white comforter with a half-dozen pillows lined up across the headboard. It's a nice room, much better than some of the hotel rooms I had been in lately.

I feel Cage come up behind me before he walks further into the room and drops our bags onto the floor. Moving to the side of the bed, he sits down and doesn't say anything. His silence is getting on my nerves, but I just want to get into the bathroom and do a shot before I have to face him.

"I brought a sexy outfit to wear for you tonight. You're going to love it!" I tell him as I pick up my bag and walk towards the open doorway into the bathroom. "I'm going to take a quick bath and get ready for you," I call out as I shut the door.

Before our addiction, this had been our thing. Back when our lives were normal, and we were falling in love, we would get home from a concert or something, and I would head to the bathroom to get ready for Cage. He loved that I dressed up for him, a surprise every time. I used to spend hundreds of dollars a month on new outfits to make him happy. Sometimes it was fishnet stockings connected to thigh-high garter belts, or rubber dresses and crotchless panties. Sometimes it was a leather corset with lacy panties or chains wrapped around my entire body. And it was always stripper shoes, high and with a sharp heel.

I drop my bag onto the bathroom floor and reach for the zipper and slide it open. I can feel a rush begin to throb through me; I'm getting excited. I'm going to do a massive shot of dope, get dressed in lingerie, and bang Cage like a dirty whore. It's a solid plan.

I eagerly search for the bag that contains my kit, but it's not near the top where I expected it to be. Frantically, I pull everything out, dropping the items to the floor in a heap. I get to the bottom of the bag, and it's empty, and I can feel panic begin to grow. Diving into the pile at my feet and examine every piece before stuffing it into my luggage. With a sick feeling, I realize that I have either left it in the car. Or worse, Cage has taken it.

I try to control the rush of violent rage that tears through me—that motherfucker has stolen my dope. I reach for the door handle, ready to walk in the room and demand that he give it back—it was mine, and I needed it. Just as I'm about to twist the knob, I stop and reconsider. That wasn't going to work; confrontation with Cage never did.

Taking a deep breath, I reach down into the pile and find the white chemise I had stolen yesterday. The edges are trimmed in lace, and the material is so thin that the outline of my nipples shows through. Slipping it over my head, I run my hands over my chest and smooth it down my body. I decide that I'm not going to waste time with lotion or looking for the matching panties and quickly slide my feet into the shiny white stilettos lying on the floor.

Anxious to get to my dope, I throw the door open and walk towards Cage. Sitting at the edge of the bed, hunched over with his elbows on his knees, he stares at the ground. I follow his gaze and see my kit lying between his feet. *Oh, shit.*

"Baby—" I start to say, but Cage cuts me off.

"Sit down," he growls, sending a shiver of dread shooting through me.

I consider ignoring him, but without dope, my confidence is

waning. And the look on his face tells me that would be a mistake. I slowly walk towards him and lower myself onto the bed, wishing I hadn't bothered with these stupid hooker shoes. I'm too scared to look at him, too ashamed to face the man I had once loved more than anything in the world.

The man I now hated because he was forcing my hand before I was ready.

I hear the memory from all those years ago reverberate inside my head and know that what I'm about to do will change everything. It will make me everything I despised in Cage because now I know precisely why Cage had shot me up; he wanted me with him, no matter the cost. He knew what would happen to me, but the selfish bastard did it anyway. He destroyed my life so he wouldn't be alone. And I'm about to return the favor.

I open my mouth to speak. "Cage, I'm sorry! I tried so freaking hard, but I can't do this without you!" I can hear the pleading in my voice and keep going, "Babe, I need you to bring me back. Just do a shot with me, and then we will both quit. It will be our last one forever, and ever, I swear!" But I knew it won't be because I don't want it to be. I'm not ready to quit, and I'd be damned if Cage is going to move on without me. He owes me.

My words drop into the silence and spread throughout the room, sliding into the dark corners and crawling up the walls. Like a sickness, they fill the air. He looks into my eyes, and I can almost see the gears in his brain move as he thinks about what I've just told him. He is forced to confront my months of untruths and deception. My lies hit him like a wrecking ball, and I can feel his fury—taste his hurt.

"You lying bitch! You. Stupid. Lying. Fucking. Bitch." His body shakes with rage, and his words are tight and threatening. "How could you do this to me? To us? You bring dope here? What the hell is wrong with you?"

In the back of my mind, I know that I should be scared. I've seen Cage pissed off before, usually at me, but I've never seen him like this. I can feel the temper and sense the violence beating through him, but I feel nothing.

His hand shoots out across the distance between us and roughly grabs me by the back of my head. Twisting his fingers through my hair, he yanks my head towards him, forcing me to my knees and between his legs. I don't make a sound; I just stare blankly up at him, broken and empty.

Cage glares back at me, boiling rage slipping out and falling down his face. I realize that he is crying. Cage never cries. I know I should feel something. Contrition, maybe? But I'm numb and can't feel anything at all. His eyes get dark and fill with grief and heartbreak.

For a second—the briefest of moments—I beg with my eyes for him to save himself. I plead for him to stand up, walk out the door, and leave me behind. I was wrong to do this to him, so damn wrong. But this is who I am now—this is the woman that he created.

I watch as the full spectrum of emotions plays out across his beautiful face. Disgust for my lying mouth, heartbreak for the life we would never have, and the hate he would always feel for me. But then I see his face break into something I can use, an emotion that I can control. I see lust and desire—but I don't want to screw him. At least, not yet. I want to get high first, and I want to get high with him.

"Baby, I already have shots ready. Please, just one, and then we can bang all night," I promise. "And tomorrow, we can go to my mom's and start our life over, together!"

He looks down at me, and I see the strain and the torment in his eyes, and I know the war has begun; I can see it written all over his face. He looks so conflicted that it would break my heart if I cared. But right now, the only thing I can hear is the devil whispering in my ear. This is Cage's fault anyway; we are here because of the choices he made. He ruined both of our lives. I don't feel regret or remorse—I feel vindicated.

I pull away from him, letting a moan of pain slip out of my mouth when I feel hair tear away from my head as I fall to the floor. I fumble around on the ground and search for the bag, finding it half-hidden under the bed. Ripping the zipper open, I pull out two rigs already loaded and ready to go. Big shots—the kind we both loved.

"Let me put water in these," I say as I walk towards the sink.

After catching a brutal case of cotton fever, I no longer bother with spoons and filters for my dope. I can't imagine anything in meth that could make me sicker than shooting the cottons had. Now, I just drop the ice directly into the syringe, add water, and shake it until it dissolves into a thick liquid.

I do this to both syringes and shake them as I walk back to Cage. I need to hurry because the spell could be broken any second, and then he might take away my drugs. Handing one to Cage, I sit down beside him and hold my breath as I watch him flip it over in his hands and examine it. I wonder if he will toss in onto the floor and crush it beneath his feet—that's what he should do—but he doesn't. He just stares at it, rotating it through his fingers one at a time.

I start getting impatient, and I remember this game from when we first started getting high together, the torture of having to wait for him to take care of me because I didn't know how to shoot myself up. But I did now, and I no longer had to wait for him.

I start examining my arms, feeling for a vein that I know isn't there because I don't have any left. But I keep up the charade because I know that Cage will be disgusted if I go straight for my feet—feet were reserved for the strung-out junkies. I was already there, but I didn't want him to know that.

I can feel his eyes on me, and the tension freaks me out. But then I feel a vein on the inside of my right wrist, next to the bone. I cringe because I've hit that bone before, more than once, and it hurts like hell. Flipping the needle backward, I aim it towards the vein. I don't hesitate; I need to get high, and I no longer care if Cage joins me or what he thinks of me. I just want to shoot before he decides we aren't doing this and takes my rig away.

Please, God, just let me hit, I beg inside my head.

I slide the tip of the needle into my skin as slowly as I can, methodically, my eyes focused intently on the base of the barrel. When I see a tiny dot of blood appear, I hook my thumb under the plunger and pull it back. I want to scream out when I see the blood rushing back, swirling to combine with the dope, but I keep completely still. I don't want to lose it. I slowly push the plunger back towards my body and watch as the thick liquid disappears into my skin. I gasp when I feel a sharp burning sensation—I have pushed through the vein and shot meth directly into my arm. The ache makes me grind my teeth and consider pulling it out and starting over. I decided to try once more, and with sweat forming at my temples, I drag the needle backward a millimeter before guiding it into my wrist from the side.

I check to make sure that I'm back in before I push the last few drops of dope and blood into the vein and sigh with relief when I see the empty barrel. I remove the needle and toss it across the room—I know what's coming, and I'm ready for it to take me.

At the injection site, a drop of blood forms, and I watch it as it falls onto the bottom of my chemise, leaving a stain like the one on my soul. I see Cage looking at it and wonder how much he must hate me right now. Immediately following that thought, I feel the dope hit my heart and begin to spread to every part of my body. A sense of well-being and warmth rolls through my chest, and I track it as it heads right down to the place between my legs.

Before my body takes over, I crawl into Cages lap, one leg on either side of his. My heart is pounding, and the vibrations of my pulse are surging and washing my desire to the surface. The throbbing ache between my legs makes me throw my head back and moan out loud. The madness inside me is rising, and I can feel the heat beating through me like an inferno that I never want to put out. Like a dog in heat, I grind my hips against Cage's dick and wrap my hands around the back of his head. Dropping my mouth, I scrape my teeth across his ear and whisper, "I need you inside of me."

Cage reacts, forcibly pushing me onto the bed; the impact sends another surge of desire racing through my body. I watch as he walks to the chair in the corner of the room and sits down, defeated. God, he is so unbelievably hot, I think. Staring at the loaded rig in his hand, he hesitates for a second and then looks over at me and says, "I hate your guts." His words are delivered with so much venom, so much scorn, I can taste his hatred land on my tongue, and I swallow it.

In response, I close my eyes, slide one hand between my legs, and start touching myself. I let my legs fall open so that Cage can watch how much his hate means to me. My other hand runs up the length of my body, sliding the virginal white teddy up and over my head before tossing it off the foot of the bed.

Cupping my hand under my right breast, I tweak my nipple between my fingers, pinching and pulling until it's rock hard.

Letting my head drop forward, I follow the tip of my pink tongue and watch it reach for the stiff peak. Flicking my tongue across the tight little pink nub, I drag it into my mouth, sucking hard. He used to love to watch me do this; it drove him crazy.

Lifting my head, I turn to face him, narrow my eyes, and throw his spite right back at him. "Fuck me like you hate me, then."

Cage isn't looking at me; he has already found his spot, right in the crook of his arm. I watch as the needle slides beneath his skin, and blood cascades into the barrel. He pauses, not moving, and I just want to scream at him to push the dope into his arm. I know that Cage is trying to find the strength to stop, but history tells me that he is powerless against dope. Holding my breath, I wait; I've already won.

Finally, his thumb moves to the back of the plunger, and the red liquid disappears into his arm. The hand between my legs moves faster, my body trembles, and my moans get louder. Once the rig is empty, he rips it out of his arm and throws it against the wall. I hear it hit before it falls silently to the floor.

Cage throws his head back and roars. I almost cum because in that sound is the dragon we have been chasing, the one we search for every time we shoot up and screw, and the dragon we look for in every person we've taken to bed after. The only time we had ever caught him was the first time. Tonight, we would have him again.

I stare as he stands and rips off his shirt and belt. His pants slip off his perfect hips and drop to the floor, and he quickly walks to the end of the bed. Flipping onto my knees, I crawl and meet him there. He stares down at me, and the demon inside my head smiles.

"Fuck me now," I demand, my words assertive, like a command. I will not beg, not this time. I feel powerful and brave.

Then I see him tense, and in a flash, his hands are on my throat, circling my neck. His fingers dig into my skin, cutting off my air.

I cannot breathe. Panic consumes me, and I grab his wrists, trying to unwrap his fingers, but he jerks me off the bed and holds me in the air. I kick and flail, and my legs try to find purchase on anything that will relieve the pressure on my throat. He is going to kill me! I stare at him, my eyes wide with shock. Cage stares back at me, and I know that the hatred I see in his eyes is reflected in mine. We didn't just teach it; we lived it, and we breathed it. Now, his soul was as dirty as mine.

With a sound of disgust, he tosses me back onto the bed, and I greedily suck in air, rage consuming me. I want to launch myself at him, scratch, and tear him apart, marking every inch of his perfect body in blood. But I feel my body betraying me; the need between my legs is growing, the voracity of my desire quickly overcoming the thoughts in my head. I look at him, my eyes burning a path straight to his, and my mouth curls into a twisted smile. He returns it with a cruel smile of his own. It's like we both understand. There would be no making love, not now, and never again. This is what we had become—two animals filled with contempt, fighting to rip each other apart from the inside out. And we reveled in it.

Cage drops onto the bed and moves over my body. Anxious to feel him against me, I grab him by the back of his head and yank him the last few inches and feel the pressure of his weight, pushing me into the bed. I try to pull his head to mine, wanting to capture his mouth and taste his lust, but he turns his head to the side, denying me.

He covers my face so he doesn't have to look at me, and in one motion, invades my body. I'm slippery wet, and ready for him. He is relentless, and I am on fire. I grab his neck and carve my nails into his throat. Feeling satisfied, I watch as the deep scratches swell with blood.

Cage rebounds with a painful jerk of my hair, yanking my head back and exposing my throat. As he pounds against me, his mouth drops to the soft skin above my collar bone and bites me. Hard. I whimper in pain and slam my open palm against the side of his face, the slap echoing around the room like a gun going off. His outrage erupts, and before I can stop him, he has captured both of my hands and trapped them over my head. I struggle to break free, but he easily blocks all of my efforts. Screaming in frustration, I wrap my legs around his waist and lock my ankles together. Pulling him deeper into me, I set our rhythm.

The sudden confinement and loss of control make Cage go crazy. He lunges backward, easily breaking my hold on him. My arms are abruptly free, but the sudden absence of him inside me drops me into desperation. As a cacophony of screams burst out of my mouth, Cage slips his hands under my ass and flips me onto my face.

I hear Cage's voice through the dark, "Get on your knees. I don't want to see your face when I fuck you." He spits on me. "You're a dirty whore, and you make me sick."

I place my hands on either side of my head and tuck my knees beneath my body and pull myself up. Shooting my ass into the air like the dirtiest of sluts, I give credence to his words—he's right, I am a whore—the one he created.

Grabbing me by the hips, Cage digs his fingers down to the bone and roughly pulls me toward him. I feel his tip rub across my sensitive nub, and I squeeze my legs, trying to keep it there. He senses what I am trying to do and reaches down and grabs a handful of my hair and yanks my head back just as he slams into me. Unforgiving, every stroke is filled with violence, and I match him, thrust for thrust. He is hurting me, trying to punish me for who I've become. Our pace is fueled by the white-hot dope beating through our veins, and our madness sustains our desire to keep going until we got off. Or until one of us is dead. Cage is ruthless and unforgiving.

I feel myself get close, my explosive orgasm rising to the surface. Slamming my eyes shut, I push all my focus towards the throbbing between my legs. I feel the cliff race toward me, and I rush to the edge and stand there, swaying. I'm on the verge of tumbling, frantic to fall into the open space, desperate to shatter and shoot my cum all over Cage. Inhaling sharply, I am almost there, like right there, and suddenly, the edge disappears, and I am back in the valley, staring up at the impossible mountain.

"Fuck," I scream in defeat. I'm covered in sweat and frustrated —I have to start over, and the disconnect from my body and the moment forces tears to start leaking from my eyes. I catch the drops with my tongue and swallow the burn.

Cage is still climbing behind me, so I redouble my efforts by putting my hands between my legs and stroking wildly. I am so dry that I have to spit into my hand and rub it between my legs, or I'll tear myself apart.

Determined to beat him to the end, I push back onto his cock, and rub myself so hard that I know I will be raw and bloody before the night is over. And I don't even care because the only thing that matters—the only thing I care about—is getting off. The room could catch on fire, and I wouldn't be able to stop.

Cage is breathing harder, the sounds coming out in short bursts. His body is slamming into me so hard that I have to fall onto my face so that I can keep my hand moving between my legs. My neck feels like it's going to break, and I know that the friction across my cheekbone will leave a scratch, scarring my face forever. I welcome it.

Cage is gasping, and his thrusts are intensifying, building right to the edge. He rocks into me frantically, and I can feel the moment that he loses his peak too. Taking his defeat out on my body, he delivers a painful smack to my ass. And then another, and another, each one more powerful than the last. I scream in pain and pleasure; I'm not sure which one dominates. The heat and blazing pain launch me back up the mountain.

"Make it hurt, please," I beg through gritted teeth. Cage does not disappoint. He destroys me, and I ride it to the edge again and scream, "Make me cum, Cage."

But he doesn't, and I don't. I can't, and neither can he—not for hours. We keep trying. Like animals, we fuck, spit, and suck. I taste blood and see it on my hands and covering my body. I'm so dry and tight that every second vibrates between unbearable hell and a desperate need to keep going. We fight our way to the edge and punish each other when we can't fall off. We scream obscenities until we can't breathe, we debase ourselves in the filthiest ways, but we keep going; the insanity never ceases.

Finally, I get there. On the rim of that mountain, my foot slips, and finally, I fall.

I'm rewarded with the most disappointing orgasm I've ever had. It feels artificial and nowhere near satisfying. The earth does not move, my world is not rocked, and the only thing dripping is the sweat and blood from hours of effort. With barely a whimper, my orgasm is gone before it even makes me moan.

I want to start again, but I need another shot first. I try to extricate myself from Cage, but he grabs me by my hair, drags me off the end of the bed, and cruelly shoves me to my knees. Towering above me, he tangles his hands into my hair and forces himself into my throat. My mouth is dry and must feel like sandpaper, but it doesn't slow him down. I stare up at him, and when our eyes catch, he spits in my face—the ultimate act of demoralization and humiliation.

Outraged, I push against the front of his thighs, trying to escape, but he is too strong. Fueled by his revulsion of me and the sickness of dope sex, he pinches the bridge of my nose so that I can't breathe and continues to ride my mouth. He won't stop this time, even if his rise and fall means that I'm going to die.

A sane man would have sensed the moment I realized that all I had to do to break free was use my teeth and slam my jaw shut. But meth sex isn't sane— it's the very definition of insanity.

Floating into my mind across tendrils of black-gray smoke, my favorite demon whispers, "Do it."

The darkness in my head takes over, and it no longer matters that I can't breathe. The panic recedes, replaced with the vision of blood showering me like rain, baptizing me and cleansing me of my sins. I find comfort in the power that I hold in my mouth. I'm about to destroy Cage in a very physical way when the pressure on my nose is gone, and I can breathe again.

Not knowing how close he had come to losing his manhood, Cage explodes with a wail of triumph. His success shoots into my mouth and hits the back of my throat, making me choke. I finally break free, and in a final act of defiance, spit his triumph back onto him with a smile.

Cage staggers to the side of the bed and sits on the edge, panting. I crawl across the floor to his feet and bow my head before him, willing him to reach down and pull me into his arms. I need him to hold me and make everything right in my head. The rush of the high has ebbed, and the culmination of everything we have done tonight hits me—and I break apart with regret.

If we were in this moment before our addictions, Cage would scoop me off the floor and lay me onto his chest, his hand covering my ears to silence the noise inside my head. He would plant kisses on my forehead and tell me that everything was okay—that we would always be okay.

Now, there is only silence between us. He falls back onto the bed, rejecting me. I want to cry, but I have nothing left. My eyes are dry, and my soul is empty.

I look towards the window and see an orange glow around the curtains' outline. It looks like the portal to hell, and I wish it would open up and welcome me home. It was morning; we had been at it all night.

Through the shadows, Cage asks, "Do you have any more?" His voice is rough and bitter.

I hesitate, trying to grab onto the last piece of decency that existed inside my conscience. I should tell him no, pack our shit, and head home. I need to do the right thing, right now, because this is my last chance. I would lose him, and I would lose myself if I didn't make the right choice.

The truth is that I have enough dope to keep us both high for days. I only had our two shots in my bag, but like a good addict—or a smart one, anyway—I have a sack of dope in my mom's car as well, hidden inside a magnetic box beneath the front seat.

The choice should be easy; nothing in my life has ever mattered more than Cage. Except for the disease that lives inside my mind.

"Yes," I whisper as our future burns.

Three days later, we walk into my mom's house, strung out and exhausted. My mom is sitting on the couch, silent, and I can't even meet her eyes. When I had finally read her text messages, I knew that she was furious. Even worse, I had broken her heart. Again—for the millionth time. She had figured out that I had been lying, that I had never been clean in the first place. She wasn't stupid—just hopeful that maybe this time I had been telling the truth.

Saying nothing, Cage and I walk into my room and shut the door. No words are spoken between us either, and fully clothed, we fall onto my bed. Moments before sleep finally pulls me under, I briefly consider crawling onto his chest. However, the three-day run we had just been on negated any possibility of me exerting that kind of effort. So, I let the darkness take me.

I'm not sure how long I sleep—hours, or maybe days—but I feel like I'm in a dream when I slowly open my eyes. It's not a noise that alerts me that I'm not alone, but a feeling. The air around me is thick and heavy. Sitting takes tremendous effort, but I force myself up.

Feeling uneasy, I peer into the dark and see a shadow form at the end of the bed. I reach for my bedside light and flick the switch. The room lights up, and the sudden flash forces me to blink my eyes. When they finally focus, I look up to see Cage standing there, still, and staring down at me.

When our eyes meet, I know that we are both seeing the same thing: regret.

I look towards the door, and dread floods me when I see his bags lying there. "Where are you going?"

Cage sits on the side of the bed, his weight rolling me towards his body. Wrapping my arms around his waist, I bury my head into his lap. I can feel his gaze on me, and I shiver when he runs his hand across my face. I pull myself closer to him, trying to stop what I know is coming. We sit there like this for a long moment, saying nothing. And then he breaks the silence—and my heart.

"Wind, I can't do this. Not again. I love you and will always love you, but I don't want this life anymore."

The world surges in front of me, and I quickly sit, apprehension building inside my gut. Turning my face so that I can look at him, I say, "Wait, what do you mean? Let's just stop then."

Agony moves across his face. "I'm leaving Wind."

"Baby, look, we have enough dope for one more shot for each of us, and then it's gone. We won't get any more, and we can do what we planned and start a new life."

Shaking his head, he looks at me with sad eyes. "It doesn't work like that, and you know it." Cage kisses me on the forehead before standing up and walking to his bags.

"You piece of shit! You would really leave me like this?!" I see red, anger pulsing through me and spilling out of every pore in my body. "You aren't going to even try to save me? You ruined my life, and you're just going to leave me here to die?"

Grief crosses his face, and his eyes fill with tears. "From the bottom of my heart, I'm sorry." He turns his back on me and walks out of the room.

Launching myself off the bed, I chase after him, hysterical. Throwing myself at his feet, I wrap my arms around his legs, attaching to him. And I start to beg.

"Please. I'm sorry. I'm so sorry. Don't go. Don't leave me." Tears burn their way down my face, and I sob into his jeans.

Cage bends down and extricates me from his legs. Once free, he quickly walks to the front door, leaving me sobbing on the ground. I cannot bring myself to stand up and chase after him because I am past the point of insanity. I pull my hair and scream incoherently. Through the fog of tears, I watch Cage pause and turn around, igniting hope that he has changed his mind. His words immediately dash that hope.

"I love you. Goodbye, Wind." With that, he slips into the night.

I throw my head back and shriek, my entire body shaking. Throwing myself onto the hard floor, I pull my legs to my chest and slam my face onto my knees. I feel pain explode in my nose and radiate across my skull. Rocking back and forth, I start moaning.

My mom comes flying into the room and rushes to me, still tying the belt of her robe. "Honey, what's wrong—are you ok?" I can barely hear her over the sound of my keening. She touches my shoulder, trying to comfort me.

Feeling her fingers unleashes another wave of fury, and I jump up and start screaming at her. "Leave me the hell alone!" She takes a step back, frightened. "I hate you Mom, and I hate my stupid fucking life!"

Turning around, I run to my room. Before I shut the door, my words stab her in the heart again.

"I hope that I die like Aaron because you don't deserve children!"

I slam the door so hard that the frame shakes. My mom is crying on the other side. I feel briefly remorseful, wondering why I always felt the need to lash out and hurt her. But the thought quickly passes as the reality of this moment hits me right in the face.

Cage had really left me. The son of a bitch had walked away, leaving me to die. There had been no attempt to save me or help me; he had just decided that his life matters more than mine. In an instant, all my will is gone. I am alone, forever stuck in the living hell that Cage had invited me to.

I throw myself onto the bed and scream into my pillow, unleashing my agony and fury. Real tears—huge beads of misery—soak my bed. The storm surges until I am completely drained. Spent and vulnerable, voices fill my head, and their whispers bring relief and comfort. "Do you really care that Cage is gone? Doesn't his absence make it easier to chase dope? Isn't this what you wanted anyway? You're free from the pressure of getting clean, and now, you can do whatever the hell you want."

And that is exactly what I do.

Over the next few weeks, all I do is get high, barely sleeping, and always screwing. I spend my nights with men and women who mean nothing and whose names are instantly forgotten. I chase the gifts of meth—the numbness, the escape, and the complete separation from any thoughts of Cage and his betrayal.

It was working until the day my phone rang with a collect call from the Dallas County Jail. Smiling, I quickly accept the charges because I know who will be on the other end of the line, and I cannot wait to gloat.

"Hello," I answer in a sing-song voice.

There's a moment of silence, then the voice speaks. "You stupid bitch—I wish I had never met you!"

"Cage, baby, why would you say that?" I laugh.

"I got caught with dope that I would never have had if you hadn't shown up with shots when I got released!" He sucks in a shaky breath. "I am totally screwed. They're going to revoke my parole and make me serve the rest of my sentence!"

A rush of pure joy moves through my sick soul. This is what he gets for leaving me—it's his punishment.

Not attempting to hide the irony in my voice, I say, "Damn, that sucks. Why didn't you just stop getting high? I mean, isn't that what you told me to do? 'Just get clean, Wind. Just stop banging dope, Wind.' Obviously, you haven't been able to do what you expected me to do, and I hope you rot in prison."

Without waiting for a response, I disconnect the call and immediately block the number. Cold satisfaction fills my soul—he deserves what he got, and I don't feel one bit of contrition. As far as I'm concerned, we're even. He ruined my life, and now I've repaid the favor.

Checkmate.

6
DOPE SEX
PRESENT DAY

Reviews from *Addict Chick: Sex, Drugs & Rock 'N Roll*

"I like an addiction book as much as the next guy, but this was unadulterated porn. She has no class." – Amazon Customer

"For some reason, I bought this without reading the reviews, and I wish I had. I am no prude, but this is absolute filth......"– Amazon Customer

"... *so not recovery*." – Amazon Customer

"I was really unsettled to find that 'Addict Chick' is a brand. It raises questions for me about the author's sincerity regarding her addiction and recovery." – Amazon Customer

"Sadly felt that this book glorifies addiction... No talk about recovery." – Amazon Customer

"She sensationalized her drug use in this book." – Amazon Customer

"There was too much gory sex and not enough about the actual addiction and recovery process." – Amazon Customer

"No way she will stay clean."– Amazon Customer

"sucked...some druggie whore trying to make some money." – Amazon Customer

"Reading this made me want to use meth so I could have sex all night."
- Amazon Customer

*P*retty brutal, huh? And those are just a few of the glowing one-star reviews on Amazon for my first book, *Addict Chick: Sex, Drugs & Rock 'N Roll*. There are plenty more; feel free to check them out. For the rest of the chapter, I'll be using the acronym SDRR for the sake of brevity—and because my editor charges per word.

Years ago, when the book was released, I had notifications set up so that Amazon would let me know when a new review had been posted. For the first few weeks, I excitedly checked my email every twenty minutes, eager to read what people thought of my first piece of literary art. I had, after all, poured my heart into the book, sharing my deepest secrets and darkest moments. It was the story of my life, written within the first year of being clean. Writing a book and carrying it over the finish line is incredibly difficult. I hadn't used a ghostwriter, couldn't afford an editor, and I published the book entirely on my own. It was the culmination of nearly a year of hard work, and I had never been more proud of anything in my life.

I learned very quickly how devastating and soul-shattering reviews could be. The negative reviews streamed in, and I was crushed. Even the good reviews weren't enough to erase the words that broke my heart. Every hateful word cut me like a razor—it was death by a thousand cuts. I cried so many tears, feeling humiliated and broken. And I was angry; offended that anybody would be so cruel, bitter that there were so many people that clearly didn't understand what the book was about, and furious that so many people with long-term recovery felt like it was okay to write a review full of judgment against another addict.

So, I had to stop reading all the reviews to save my sanity, but the criticisms never left me. The harsh opinions of a few created persistent insecurity for me, and it would be a very long time before I found the courage to write another book. I never rechecked the reviews until about ten minutes ago when I began writing this chapter. I always knew that I would include them in this book to address parts of my first book. Still, I dreaded the moment I would have to go back on Amazon, click the single star button, and face my most immense torment.

There are more than there used to be, and they still sting just as much as they did back then. But nearly five years after writing SDRR, I realized that those negative reviews were right. At least, some of them; there are still some written by assholes who want to slam my grammar, and they don't even know the difference between "your" and "you're." And the ever-present sanctimonious recovery elite who have it all figured out, gleefully leaving a review on how I am recovering all wrong because I'm not doing it the way they are. And for the people that declared that I would never stay clean: here I am, nearly six years later, still clean.

The reviews about how I glorified addiction and romanticized the sex, however, were mostly accurate. I want to take this chapter in Addict Chick unCaged to explain a few things, apologize for a few more, and throw myself on your mercy.

I began writing SDRR when I was just a few months clean. It was never meant to be a book about recovery—I didn't even understand the meaning of the word yet. I suppose the argument could be made that I had no business writing a memoir about my life as an addict so soon after getting clean, but I would argue that writing that book saved my life. And it certainly had a significant impact on the life I am living today.

To explain my motivations for writing the book the way I did, I've had to do a lot of soul-searching. It's important to me that I get this part right. I've tried to analyze it as objectively as possible—scrutinizing the content and how I chose to describe certain situations—and discovered that the woman I was when I wrote that book is far different than the one who is writing this one. If I were writing SDRR today, it wouldn't be the same book. Over half a decade has passed; time brings clarity, and reflection brings perspective.

Yet, if I could go back and write SDRR over again, would I? No, because it was an honest depiction of the way I remembered active addiction to be, at a time when I was still coming to terms with everything that had happened. And that will resonate—has resonated—with many women just getting clean or new to recovery. The way we recollect our addiction during the first year isn't always the way we remember it when we hit two, three, four, or five years of clean time. At least, that's been my experience.

That is the real reason I've included this chapter—to explain and acknowledge that I made a huge mistake when I wrote SDRR. Particularly when it comes to sex, most notably, dope sex. The reviews were correct; I did glorify it, and I was wrong. The way I had remembered and the way I wrote about sex on meth wasn't exactly the way it really was. There is a psychological term for it: euphoric recall, the tendency for people to remember past experiences positively while overlooking the negative experiences associated with that event. It's relatively common for people that suffer from substance abuse.

I cringe when I read some of the stuff I wrote in SDRR, and I can see why so many people were repulsed. I mean, it did read like erotica—and not even good erotica! The original draft of unCaged included graphic sex, but I removed most of it—I do not want to be considered an author who writes smut. The only reason I left in the scene you just read in chapter five was to attempt to adequately explain what dope sex was really like, not the way I wanted to remember it. If you've read SDRR, then you would recognize the sex you just read is much different than the sex I wrote in SDRR.

Just to be extremely clear, so there isn't any confusion, dope sex is revolting. Everything about it is disgusting. It is not glamorous, romantic, or sexy; it's ugly, gross, and it will twist your mind up in the sickest ways. It will make you do things that never in a million years—even in your worst nightmares—could you ever imagine doing. I had sex with a sixty-year-old man with no teeth, and I thought he was sexy. I banged a guy on the floor of a trailer that had no running water or electricity, surrounded by rat shit and stray dogs. Dope sex is hours and hours spent chasing after an orgasm that never comes. There is not one single thing about sex on dope that I miss—not one. Even if the only sex I could ever have again in my life had to be dope sex, I would rather be a nun. Or die.

For the last five years, I have been torn apart by people based on SDRR and how I wrote it. I have lived with this nagging feeling of shame over that book, with the constant need to defend my words. I've been told that I was an embarrassment to recovery and that I should be ashamed of myself and my book. I let the world decide that I was a terrible writer and tear apart my dream of being an author. And it all began with those one-star reviews.

Today, after all these years, I also read the five star reviews for the first time. I should have been reading them all along because they are the people I wrote the book for.

"Amanda opened her life to readers not just to help her heal, but to help others realize they, too, can overcome their demons." – Amazon Customer

"I am looking at it from a mother's standpoint. I loved it and thought you really captured what my kid has gone thru. I am so proud of you for getting clean!" – Amazon Customer

"Eye opening account of addiction and the road to get there." – Amazon Customer

"What a life. I thought I was reading a replica of my own." – Amazon Customer

"She gives me such hope!" – Amazon Customer

"I couldn't imagine what it took to write a book like this." – Amazon Customer

"This is one of the best 'in your face' books..." – Amazon Customer

"I was unable to put it down as her writing style is very creative and raw" – Amazon Customer

"Even girls that haven't struggled with substance abuse can generally relate to being addicted to love..." – Amazon Customer

"If you haven't loved like that or had sex like that... I truly feel sorry for you!" – Amazon Customer

"She completely opens herself up to share her story, which is both admirable and inspiring!" – Amazon Customer

"She is a brave and talented writer." – Amazon Customer

"Love her, love the book, love the truth, love that we are all trying to break the stigma." – Amazon Customer

"Just wanted to thank her for sharing this with the world because it's ALWAYS good to know someone else felt what I felt, and I'm not alone!" – Amazon Customer

"She hid nothing." – Amazon Customer

"There was so much in this book that I related to in my own addiction that I thought no one else would understand." – Amazon Customer

"To the people who felt like the sex was gratuitous, you need to do more research on addiction. The sex addiction was part of her story, and I'm glad she told it" – Amazon Customer.

"I can connect with her on so many levels..." – Amazon Customer

"I often shook my head at how close our story is." – Amazon Customer

"I admire her strength & honesty!" – Amazon Customer

No, I have no regrets about writing *Addict Chick: Sex, Drugs & Rock 'N Roll.*
None.

7

MOTHERS, DAUGHTERS, AND SONS

Dear Cage,

Heading to Kentucky! I can't wait to see Mason! He doesn't know I'm coming, and I'm excited to see the look on his face when he sees me!

  I'm glad I at least got to talk to you before I left, even though I wish I had been able to see you. It's driving me crazy that you haven't seen me clean in so long, but I understand why you didn't want me to come. I AM sorry for what happened last time, more sorry than you will ever know. You don't know how often I have wished I could go back to that day, or back to the very beginning, and make different choices. There are so many things I would have done differently; I need you to know that.

Leaving Texas is hard only because I am leaving you. We've finally both made our lives right, and now I'm going to be twelve hours away from you. I don't know what will happen with us, but I know that our story isn't over. Not even close. You always told me that we would be okay, I believed it then, and I believe it now.

I read an Edgar Allan Poe quote yesterday, and it reminded me of us:

"We loved with a love that was more than love."

Please write me back; my new address in Kentucky is on the envelope. I love you!

Love,
    Wind

P.S. Wish me luck — I hope I don't screw this mom thing up!

"You better get to work. Those boxes won't unpack themselves," my mom says as she walks into the room.
I'm sitting on the hardwood floors in the middle of my living

room with my arms wrapped around my knees. Surrounded by unopened boxes, I stare down at a picture of my kid. He is wearing a baby blue polo shirt with dark jeans; his little face turned towards the camera with just a hint of a smile. Bright cerulean eyes peer up at me, so much like his father's.

My heart catches when I think back to the day this picture was taken. We were at the Dallas Aquarium, having a family outing, wholesome and normal. My mom was there, shooting a million pictures and driving us all crazy, but as a Nana, she lived for that stuff. My brother and I watched our sons play, and I remember being grateful that they would grow up together. My husband was there, and we took turns holding Mason up to the glass enclosures, pointing out the brightly colored fish and wacky-looking sea life. We all laughed when a shark swooped by, scaring the shit out of him.

I stare back down at the picture and try to remember how old he was. He is wearing a diaper, so I guess maybe two? To be honest, I can't remember how old Mason was when he was finally potty trained, or when he took his first steps, or even when he said 'mama' for the first time. Milestones that moms always know. Even forty-five years later, my mom can recall the first time each of her children slept through the night and what our favorite foods were.

Once upon a time, I was a mom like that. Now, the memories of Mason as a baby seem lost, destroyed by years of drug use.

If I had known that I would lose those memories forever, would I have gotten high that first time? Or continued to get high? If I had known the full consequences of my choices, would I have still made the choices I did? These thoughts torture me when I'm alone.

I'd like to believe that I would have been smart or strong enough to walk away if I had known. But once I started getting high, the choice no longer seemed like it was mine to make. There hadn't been anything more important than getting high, not even my child.

If ever there was a statement that can explain the power of addiction, it would be this; the love that I had for my son wasn't enough to make me quit.

What a terrible thing to say, I know. And it's a statement that I could never have imagined saying or truly understood until I had lived it. If there is one thing I am absolutely sure of, it's that before my addiction, I was a damn good mother. I loved Mason so much that I would have died for him without hesitation. There is nothing in the world that he could ever do that would make me stop loving him. But there was something that could make me forget about that love and what it meant, and its name was meth.

On the left side of the picture, partially cropped out, is a woman. She has long hair that looks like burnished copper, a big nose, and she isn't wearing any makeup. Her arm is raised near her face, hand in a loose fist, with fingernails that aren't painted. She is smiling down at the little boy, and you can tell that she is genuinely happy. The woman is me, of course, but she looks nothing like me. Everything about the woman in the picture is the complete antithesis of the woman I am now. I don't look like a mom anymore, and I certainly haven't been one in years.

"Mom, what if I can't do this?" My voice is quiet, and I look up at her.

"Do what, baby?"

"Be a mom again. I have no idea what I'm doing. I don't even know how to cook!" I'm not sure why knowing how to cook is so important; I had never cooked, but it seems like it's something that good moms do. At least, that's what it looks like on Pinterest.

"Honey," my mom laughs, "I don't know how to cook, and you turned out okay. I mean, you're still alive, aren't you?"

"This isn't funny, mom! What if I screw up? What if Mason hates me?" Panic bubbles up, and I suddenly wonder who the hell thought this was a good idea. Who in their right minds thought that I should be given the responsibility of a kid? Just four months ago, I was sitting on the floor in a nasty gas station bathroom, slamming dope. The very real implications of what could go wrong and the damage I could cause, especially to my kid, makes me want to throw up.

"Calm down, you're going to be just fine," my mom sighs. "Being a mom is kind of like riding a bike!"

"Really, mom?" I roll my eyes. "The best you got is a modified Albert Einstein quote?"

"I didn't know Einstein said that! But the truth is, honey, nobody knows how to be a mom. We're all just kind of winging it." Grabbing a box cutter off the counter, she walks back to me and sits down. "Look, Mason is going to be thrilled that you're here. He loves you! The only thing you need to focus on is staying off the drugs and spending time with him. It's exactly what you need."

"What if I can't stay clean, though? What if I screw up and fail?" I look up and see my mom staring intently at me, and I know she is searching my face for some indication that I am already using. "Mom, you would know if I had already relapsed. Besides the fact that we have been together every single moment for the last couple of weeks, I've been stuffing my face with so much food that you should have no doubt."

Relief crosses her face.

"I guess I'm just scared that when you leave and go back to Texas, I will be here alone, with nobody to help me," I tell her.

"You aren't alone, silly. You will have Mason and Tempest. And Daniel is right down the road."

Daniel is Mason's father, and he is cautiously optimistic about the entire situation—if a little apprehensive. More than anything, he wants me to be clean and in Mason's life. But I've put him through hell, and it's going to take a lot to earn back his trust.

"Sweetheart, you come from a long line of strong Robertson women. We're made from sturdy stock. It's the men in our family that can't get it together." Cutting the tape off the box between us, she pulled out the new sheets and comforter set we had ordered before leaving Texas. "So, stop whining, and let's go make the bed."

We head upstairs, and twenty minutes later, I am staring at my new bed. I take in the duvet's black and white chevron pattern and wince at all the pillows lining the headboard. Millions upon millions of pillows stacked up and spread out, covering nearly every square inch of the king-size bed. Why do women do this? I honestly have no idea, but we all do it. I learned it from my mom, who learned it from her mom, and on and on. I guess since I don't have a daughter, I will be breaking the generational cycle. Maybe one day, a world will exist where women aren't required to drown their linens with flair and bullshit that ends up on the ground anyway. I decide on the spot that as soon as my mom leaves, those pillows are going under the bed, where they will stay until the next time she graces Kentucky with her presence.

I look around the room and say, "Thank you, Mama. For real."

My mom throws a black belt level karate chop onto the center of one of the pillows. "For what?"

"For everything. For getting me this place and moving me here." My eyes sting with tears, and I start to get a little choked up. "For buying me furniture. But mostly for getting me help when I asked you for it. I wouldn't have gotten clean if it hadn't been for you."

"Yes, you would have. Your hair was falling out, and we both know that was reason enough for you to get clean," she joked. "Honey, you are my daughter, and I'm going to do everything I can to help you. I wish I had the money to buy you everything you need, but it's enough to get you started."

It's more than enough, and I'm incredibly fortunate. I feel like I won the birth lottery when I think about the mom I have. Many people that I've met recently are alone in the world, literally—people who have families that won't speak to them or have no family at all. Most lack any financial resources, yet many turn their lives around. Despite the struggle and the odds stacked against them, they fight, and they make it. I find their determination to build a better life for themselves to be highly inspiring and courageous.

Not for the first time, I wonder if I would have been able to get clean without my mom and family's support. Would I have been able to start my life over at the Salvation Army, taking the bus to work every day for as long as it took to pull together the money for a place of my own? To rebuild my credit enough to be able to put a utility bill in my name? I honestly don't know if I would have been strong enough, but I'm glad I don't have to find out.

"You need to know that this will be the only time I will do this," my mom says. "If you relapse or decide to go back to that life, you will be on your own." Her words send a chill into my gut. "I will still love you, and I won't ever give up on you, but financially, I will not be able to help you like this again."

The weight of her words scares me. I understand what this had cost her; She had drained her retirement account to put me through treatment, move me to Kentucky so I could be with my kid, and to rent and furnish this beautiful townhouse.

But as I study her face from across the sea of pillows that separate us, I realize that the real cost and most significant potential for damage would be what I would do to her heart if I throw away the chance she had given me. I know in the way that I know the sun rises in the east and sets in the west that losing me again would destroy her.

On both my mom's and dad's side, my family would make a solid case study on addiction's genetic predisposition. Not too long ago, my mom and I had counted the number of people in our family that had died of overdoses or complications from years of alcohol abuse. The numbers were staggering.

On my mom's side, starting with only my grandparent's generation, including just first and second cousins, there have been twelve deaths. Not to mention the countless family members that are actively using or have at one point struggled with addiction. On my dad's side, we have lost my grandmother, my father, and my brother. I'm sure there are more, but I don't have a clear history beyond my immediate family because it isn't something we've discussed.

In the old days, the disgrace surrounding addiction and alcoholism would put the stigma we face today to shame. Back then, you just swept it under the rug and pretended it wasn't happening.

I'm not sure what cruel twist of fate had decided that my father would have four out of five of his children addicted to drugs and that my mom would have three out of three, but I guess that was just the hand they had been dealt. Of course, my father *had* been an addict for my entire life. There was always a high probability that at least one of his offspring would follow his path—he got four. But my mom was normal. She had a margarita a few times a year and usually fell asleep at the table. And the only drugs she had ever done was smoke a little pot and drop a few tabs of acid in the '70s.

I suppose with our familial history, the odds were stacked against us before we were even born. But what does that mean for our own children? Are they destined to grow up and be addicts like their parents? Have we diluted our junkie gene pool effectively enough with the partners we've chosen to procreate with? Well, statistically speaking, it's not looking good. Between myself and my four siblings, we have nine children. So far, two of them have struggled with addiction. The other seven are under the age of sixteen.

The very thought that Mason may one day grow up and become an addict is a nightmare. Having lived that life and knowing what I know now, there are very few things I can imagine that would be worse than that. Not only because I now understand the true misery of addiction, but because I also grasp the price that is paid by the family. Especially the mothers of addicts. They pay with pieces of their soul.

For as long as I can remember, my mom has battled addictions that weren't even her own. Her mother had been an addict that overdosed before I was born. She married my father, her high school sweetheart, and he was an alcoholic. And then, she went to war with my brother's addiction.

Aaron was her firstborn, and he began to get into trouble with drugs when he was in middle school. He even got expelled in the seventh grade for selling pot out of his locker. He was out of control, and my mom was determined to "fix" him. She consulted with doctors, made him see a shrink, and made us all go to family therapy. She joined support groups and read every book she could find, and there wasn't a rehab in our entire city that she didn't send my brother to.

Desperate to help him, her enabling turned into unhealthy codependency, and eventually, she became as sick as he was. When Aaron was eighteen, my mom found out that he let our other brother, Brian, experiment with marijuana. Terrified that Brian was going to follow in the steps of our brother, she made the tough decision to do whatever she could to protect him. She packed up our life and moved us to Texas, leaving Aaron behind in California.

But even a geographical change wasn't going to be enough to overcome the power of genetics. Although his addiction progressed much slower than Aarons, it wasn't long before Brian was breaking our mother's heart too.

In 2008, my mom received the call, the one that we expected might come one day but could never truly be prepared for. Aaron was dead from a suspected overdose. In Los Angeles, he had died in the arms of the police officer that had found him on the street.

Aaron was dead, Brian continued to get high, and I sat on my high horse, judging them both. I watched my mom fall apart; the stages of grief so potent that you could feel her pain just by looking at her. By the time she had hit the acceptance stage, she was different—changed in the way I imagine most women who bury a child change. A part of her heart was missing, gone forever, and nothing would ever be the same for her again.

It made me hate my brother for being an addict, dying, and not being strong enough just to quit using drugs. If not for himself, at least for our mother. She didn't deserve what he put her through; she was practically a saint. In my mind, it was that simple.

Three years later, at the age of thirty-four, I would complete the sibling trifecta, and I would find out how very wrong I had been. My addiction would open a new level of hell for my mom. I would watch her suffer, and I would feel nothing. No longer protected by the thin veil of denial that overdose only happened in *other* families, she now had irrefutable evidence that *we* were that family, confirmed by the urn of ashes that sat on top of the fireplace mantle in her living room.

"I'm not going to relapse," I promise her, "or throw this chance away." I mean every word. There would be a special place in hell reserved just for me if I was lying.

Smiling, my mom says, "I know you aren't." Her confidence and faith in me are reflected in her pale blue eyes. "Go grab your keys. It's time to get going."

I pull my phone from my pocket and glance at the time, ecstatic to see that she's right. The moment I have been waiting for since the day I got clean is finally here.

We both rush downstairs, and I grab the blue gift bag sitting on the kitchen counter before heading to my mom's car. Sliding behind the wheel, I put the key in the ignition and wait for my mom to climb in.

"Hurry up, girlfriend," I say, trying not to sound as impatient as I felt.

"I'm an old woman—this is as fast as I can go," she retorted.

Rolling my eyes, I laugh at that ridiculous statement. My mother can rock a tool belt, use a table saw, and drive a U-Haul truck across the country better than I can.

Less than five minutes later, I am pulling into the driveway at Daniel's house. He must have been watching from the window because we are just getting out of the car when I see him walking towards us, smiling.

Hugging my mom, he asks, "How is the unpacking going?"

"Well, there are boxes everywhere, but we managed to put together the bed in Mason's room," I say proudly. "I can't wait for Mason to see it. You should come by and check it out."

"I'm sure he will love it. Let me know if you guys need help with anything. The bus will be here in a few minutes. If you want, you can go across the street and wait for him. I'll stay here with your mom so that you can have a few minutes alone."

I look at my mom, and when she nods in agreement, I quickly cross the street. Feeling the warmth of the sun on my shoulders, I walk a few feet up the sidewalk and stop beside a beautiful magnolia tree to wait. Waxy green leaves rustling in the breeze, and the fragrant smell of the white blossoms reminds me that it's almost summer. Pulling in a deep lungful of air, I let the smell wash over me. The scent of a magnolia tree is so quintessentially southern that it feels familiar, and that calms me slightly.

I glance across the street at my mom and Daniel, and they are both staring at me. I watch their lips move and wonder what they are talking about. *Are they worried about how Mason will react when he sees me?* I wish Daniel had told Mason that I would be here today, but he said he wanted it to be a surprise. I went along with it, but I think it was more than likely that he didn't want to get Mason's hopes up, just in case I didn't make it. I can't say that I blamed him. The last four years have been full of deceit, broken promises, and so much heartache. I'm lucky that I'm even being allowed this chance now. *God knows I don't deserve it.*

It's not natural for a woman to be separated from her child, and it has been over six months since I have seen mine. At the tail end of my addiction, I hadn't seen him at Christmas, and then I entered treatment and missed his tenth birthday. It wasn't the first birthday I had missed, but I am going to make sure that it was the last one.

Glancing anxiously down the road, I watch as a bright yellow school bus slowly turns onto the street and heads in my direction. I can feel my heart race when it passes by me, the smell of diesel overpowering the scent of the magnolia. I stare intently into the half-open windows, searching for the face of the little boy that will, for the second time, change my life

The bus slows to a stop twenty yards in front of me. I fight the overwhelming urge to rush to the door like a psycho, knowing it would freak Mason out. My fingernails digging into the palm of my hand, I hang back as kids start appearing on the bottom step of the bus. One by one, they hop out through the open door and land on the street. I'm beginning to worry that maybe I missed him when I spot a mop of white-blonde hair shining against the sun and watch as he jumps down and walks towards the sidewalk.

My breath catches when I see his sweet face, and I wrap my arms around my chest so that my heart doesn't fall out.

The baby that I held in my arms for hours, that I watched crawl at my feet before he learned how to take his first steps, had suddenly become the little boy that is walking towards me now. He looks so damn cute in his red superhero t-shirt and jeans, and I smile when I see the backpack hanging from his shoulders. It's huge and dwarfs his small frame. I briefly wonder if Daniel bought the wrong size or if Mason had asked for an adult size bag. *Another moment in his life I've missed.*

I stand there, just staring at him, trying to burn every movement, every shift of his body and tilt of his head, into my mind. I want to memorize the slope of his neck and the tip of his nose. I want to store away the memory of the way his hair curls around the lobes of his ears and the perfect pink of his lips.

This was my baby, my son, my only child, and I haven't understood the enormity of what I had lost or what my addiction had cost until this exact second. The realization that there were a million memories that I had missed with Mason—time I could never get back—is the most gut-wrenching and devastating moment of my life. I want to beg God to let me go back to a time before I had ever met Cage and make a different choice. Because the truth, the heartbreaking reality, is that the love I had for Cage wasn't even close to the kind of love that I feel for my son.

Regret slips out of my eyes and runs down my cheeks, a river of grief burning a hole in my heart. Quickly, I wipe the back of my hand across my face, rubbing the tears away. I do not want Mason to see me sad or upset.

I focus on his face, willing him to look at me. My heart is doing cartwheels in my chest, and I am about to sprint toward him when I see his eyes land on me. I hold my breath as he hesitates, stops, then slowly turns his head back in my direction. Confusion furrows his brow, his blue eyes flash to my brown ones, and I can see the moment his brain catches up to the image inside his head.

"Mommy!" he yells, the word landing right in the center of my soul. The look on his face changes from shock to wonder, and I watch as he bolts towards me, arms outstretched. He runs along the grassy verge so that he can pass the kids that are still walking on the sidewalk, his huge backpack slipping off his shoulders and landing in his wake.

Seconds later, he leaps from the ground, sails through the air, and lands right in my waiting arms. I feel his little hands around my neck as I pull him close to me, and his skinny legs wrap around my waist and settle on the top of my hips. It's a perfect fit. He smells like peanut butter and jelly sandwiches and sunshine. Our hearts beat together, the way I used to imagine they did when he was inside my belly.

If I ever need a reminder of why fighting to stay clean is worth it, I only need to think of this moment.

Before pushing down a new wave of tears, I manage to exclaim, "My baby!"

"I'm not a baby no more, Mama," Mason laughs

The truth of his words makes my heart bleed. "You will always be my baby," I whisper, squeezing him tight.

Placing his hands on my shoulders, Mason pushes his body back until our faces are inches apart. I stare at him, thanking God for making me his mom and giving me another chance.

"Are you staying this time like you promised?" His voice is hopeful.

One of the most important jobs of being a mother is protecting your children and keeping them safe. Not only had I failed at both, but I had also been the cause of my child's suffering. For nearly half of his life, I broke Mason's heart with empty promises and confused him with my long absences and erratic behavior.

Learning to be a mom again is going to be difficult; I know that. It will test me and evolve me, and I am going to screw up. Probably a lot. But the only mistake that I could make that would be unforgivable is picking up dope. There would be no coming back from that.

With Mason still in my arms, I walk towards his dropped backpack. "Not only am I staying," I say, "but you get to come and see your new bedroom today. You can even stay the night if you want!"

"Okay, but I have to ask my dad first," he said, wriggling out of my arms before landing on the ground.

I hate to let him go, wanting to carry him around forever. "I think he will be okay with it," I say, having already asked and been answered, "but let's go ask him anyway."

Bending down, I scoop his bag off the ground and sling it over my shoulder. As we walk down the sidewalk, Mason grabs my hand, and I wonder how much longer I have until he stops doing that. I hope that it will be at least a few years before I notice that he doesn't do it anymore.

I smile and squeeze his hand, content that there is nowhere in the world I would rather be, and nobody I would rather be with than Mason.

8

MOTHERHOOD

A couple of weeks later, when the newness has worn off, and the realities of motherhood come crashing down, I change my mind. Standing in the kitchen, watching Mason play his video games, I consider running away. Or at least hiding in the closet.

I don't remember parenting being this stressful or exhausting. And I used to have to do it while working fifty-hour weeks. Maybe it was because Mason was a baby and barely spoke back then; I could pick him up, put him where I wanted, and make him do what I said. At least, I think I could. But now, he has a voice and an opinion, and he isn't scared to use them.

Bracing myself for the argument that has happened every night this week, I say, "Time to hit the sack, kiddo."

"Not tired," he says, without looking up. "Thirty more minutes."

"Mason, it's time for bed. You have school tomorrow. I have to take Nana to the airport early, and we are going to bed," I declare, feeling proud of myself for laying down the law like a boss.

Silence. No response and no movement to indicate that he was listening to me. Sitting down on the barstool behind me, I feel my confidence wane.

My mom gave me parenting advice last night. "You can't give in to him," she had said. "When you bargain or give him his way, you are teaching him how to manipulate you. You have to be firm".

"But Mom, I feel like he is going to be mad at me. I don't want to argue with him or upset him," I had replied.

I'm screwing this all up. The things that I know I *should* be doing as a mother seem to be in constant conflict with what I feel like I am *capable* of doing. I feel so guilty all the time—guilty for being away from him and scared that I'm going to do or say the wrong things. Deep down, I feel like I haven't earned the right to discipline him.

"Mason, I'm exhausted, and it's time for bed. Get your butt upstairs," I say, trying my best to sound stern.

"Just lay down on the couch and go to sleep, then. I'll wake you up when I finish playing."

God, why does he have to sound so logical? So reasonable? My eyes flick to the couch, and I briefly consider taking his suggestion. I manage to steel myself instead. "I said, it's time for bed!"

"Nope."

Tell me that that little shit didn't look straight at me and dead-ass say that.

I cross the distance between us in less than a second. Startled, Mason looks up at me. I reach down, grab the gaming device, and tear it out of his hands. "Get. The. Fuck. Upstairs." I growl as my frustration boils over into temper.

Shock and horror cross over his little face, and tears well in his eyes.

Oh, God, what have I done? I feel sick. I've made Mason cry. I can't believe I cursed at him; Daniel will be so mad when he finds out! A million thoughts are racing through my mind, and I feel real fear. What if Daniel won't let me see him anymore? What if Mason tells his teachers, and they call CPS? What in the world is wrong with me?

As Mason's wails get louder and more intense, I struggle to think of how to fix this. So, I drop on the couch and try to drag him into my arms, apologizing all over myself. He pulls away from me, and I can see that he is scared—scared of me! Pangs of guilt shoot through me, and I start to cry too. I'm not sure who's crying harder or louder, but we wake my mom, and she came down the stairs.

"What in the world is going on?" she says.

Mason jumps off the couch and shoots across the room into my mom's arms. Between hiccupping sobs, Mason manages to get out, "Nana, my mama said a bad word and yelled at me."

I hear my mom gasp and feel her gaze on me. Pleading with her eyes, I know she wants me to say there was a mistake. I just sit there, tears falling down my face, and don't say anything. What can I say? I know I handled tonight all wrong, and Mason will probably need more therapy because of me.

I quickly cross the room and lean down to talk to Mason. "Bud, I am so sorry I lost my temper. I shouldn't have yelled or cursed at you." I start rubbing his back, trying to calm us both down. "I love you, please don't be mad at me."

He doesn't reply, but his crying slows down. My mom jumps in and says, "I think we're all exhausted. It's been a rough few weeks. Let's get a good night's sleep, and we'll feel better in the morning."

"Can I sleep with you, Nana?" Mason asks.

My mom glances at me, her brow furrowed. Mason has been sleeping with me since the day we moved in. Letting him sleep with me probably hasn't been the best idea, and it would eventually make it difficult to get him into his own bed, but I haven't cared. I love sleeping next to him. Watching him makes me happy, and I feel like I can keep him safer if he's with me. Safe from what? I don't know. But the selfish part of me knows that I let him sleep with me so that I'm not alone.

"How about if we all three sleep together in your mama's bed? It's big enough, and this is my last night here; we can have a little slumber party."

"Okay..." Mason replies, reluctantly.

I smile at my mom, grateful that she was able to defuse the situation with all of her mama wisdom. We march upstairs, and with Mason between us, climb into bed. Before I fall asleep, I feel his little hand reach for mine, and I know that everything will be okay.

"I am so proud of you."

We're at the Lexington airport, standing at the entrance of the security line. My mom has her arms wrapped around my waist, hugging me close. With my face buried in the crook of her neck, I take in the familiar scent of her signature perfume, sweet vanilla sugar.

"What if I can't do this?" I ask.

She steps back so that she can look at me. "You *are* going to do this. Lean on Jesus to guide you and pray for direction. He will not leave you."

I have some doubts about this advice because praying isn't as easy as it sounds. I don't think I'm doing it right. Like, I can hear myself inside my head, and I feel stupid. Do I speak like I'm writing a letter? "Dear God..." And then ask for help, or what? Or do I talk like we're having a conversation? Should it be a formal or casual chat? See, it's confusing, and I have questions.

I try to put on a brave face. I don't want to make her worry, but I'm scared. I'm not ready to be on my own. I fear that I won't be able to silence the demons that roar inside my head if she isn't here. I had left people, places, and things behind when I moved to Kentucky, but I know that I can find dope anywhere if I want it.

My lower lip begins to tremble, and tears leak out and start falling down my face before I can stop them. Ugh. The ugly cry, and it's the worst. I feel myself flush, my eyes slim into slits like I just smoked a bowl of indica, and snot starts free fallin' from my nose like Tom Petty.

"Honey, I promise it's going to be okay. You will spend time with Mason, get your house settled, and when you're ready, you will find a job. You need to stay busy." She smiles through tears of her own. "Now, pull yourself together. You look ugly."

I laugh and walk back into her arms for a final hug.

"I love you, Mom. Thank you for everything," I say as she squeezes me tightly.

"I love you too, honey. I'll call you when I get home."

I watch as she winds through the turnstiles and makes her way to the TSA agent to hand over her documentation. I chuckle through my tears when she takes off her shoes; her socks don't match. As she passes through the airport scanners, I want to shout for her to come back and beg her not to leave me. Wrapping my arms around myself, I stare until I can't see her anymore. I feel like my security blanket is being cruelly ripped away, and all I want is my mama.

I'm alone, and it's terrifying.

Over the next few weeks, I rotate between being June Cleaver, the mom of the year who has all the answers to Peggy Bundy, the mom who can't cook for shit but still rocks a sexy wardrobe to Joan Crawford from *Mommie Dearest*. Calm down, I have never beaten Mason's ass with a wire hanger, but there have been a few times I came close. Nobody can drive me crazier than my son. I've decided that while my drug addiction didn't take me out, there is still a good chance that my kid will be the death of me.

Staying busy hasn't been a problem, but frustration certainly has. I can't seem to get anything done. Everything I try to do is so complicated and takes so long that I usually just quit and move on to something else. I open a box and never finish unpacking it, and now my house is littered with half-empty boxes. The new kitchen table my mom ordered is lying on the floor, halfway put together. I will wash a load of laundry and then end up rewashing it two or three more times because I forgot to put it in the dryer.

It's crazy because my behavior on dope was very similar to what's happening to me now. The irony is not lost on me. I would bet the ten dollars sitting in my bank account that anybody that has used meth, or been around somebody that has, knows exactly what I am talking about.

The difference between when I was actively using and now is that I'm aware that my brain function is screwed up. I knew even before I entered treatment that I would struggle for a long time after getting clean, a fact my doctors in rehab confirmed. I learned that it could take up to eighteen months before my critical thinking skills and cognitive impairments would improve to baseline levels. There was even a chance that there may be some irreversible damage and parts of who I used to be may never return,

Now that I'm here, living in these moments from hell, I have a genuine understanding of why meth is such a devastating drug. And why so many people relapse. The bleak months ahead of me feel like a dusty road leading to nowhere. Logically, I know that meth didn't make me smarter, but I know I remember feeling like I could accomplish more than what I'm able to complete now. Happiness on dope is synthetic, it's not real, but somehow that seems preferable to the way I feel now, empty and dead. Meth doesn't change what you are physically or mentally capable of doing, but it sure as hell changes the way you view the world and what you *think* you are capable of doing.

I'm not craving the high from meth; I'm craving the escape—and staying clean is going to be hard as hell.

Despite my internal struggles and daily challenges, I know I will never forget this time with Mason. We're setting a foundation that we can build from, and I've been given a chance to repair the bond between us. I'm thankful that this season of my life happened when it did because when you're stuck in active addiction, it seems like time just disappears. I could have easily lost this chance to have a relationship with my son. I know that is the fate for so many women that struggle with substance abuse; I'm going to make sure that it will not be mine.

I take at least a million pictures a day, driving Mason crazy. At night, with my son tucked in beside me sleeping, I scroll through the photos and replay every moment. One day, I will get my Martha Stewart on and figure out how to scrapbook.

We laugh all the time and do ridiculous things. We have water gun fights during the day and play video games all night. I chase after him on his skateboard and try not to freak out when he climbs trees. I watch the *Transformers* movies with him at least a hundred times. He teaches me how to play basketball, and I dunk on his ass every chance I get.

Okay, no, not really. My ass is getting so big on account of the strawberry pop-tarts I can't stop eating that I'm lucky I can jump at all. He takes advantage of my lack of knowledge for the game and makes up the rules as we go. Always to his advantage. And I let him.

We go to the fair, eat cotton candy until we're sick, and ride nearly every ride on the midway. We play the balloon and dart game, and I win him a teddy bear. That night, I watch him sleep with it tucked under his arm and thank God for letting me be his mom.

He asks me silly questions a million times a day, but I never get tired of hearing him call me Mommy. I know I get carried away and spoil him too much, but for all the moments I have missed, and all the time I can never get back, I tell myself that it's forgivable.

There are some challenging moments; times that I fail and make a lot of mistakes. Usually, those mistakes come from my inability to regulate the emotions that seem to come and go as they please. Or from overestimating my problem-solving abilities. There are times that Mason needs help with his electronics and sits on the floor, crying. Having no idea how to fix it, I sit on the floor and cry with him.

I start following the Stepford Wives on Pinterest and attempt to roll out a chore chart with stupid star stickers and everything. Mason looks at me like I'm crazy. "Mom, I'm not even tall enough to reach the buttons on the washing machine. What is an iron anyway?" The chart ends up in the garbage not long afterward—a checkmark in the 'mom fail' column.

There are moments that I know I nail the mom thing for sure, though.

Like, I'm aware that letting him eat candy for breakfast isn't a good idea, so after letting him eat sour patch kids with his milk, I buy him Lucky Charms the next time I'm at the grocery store. See, I'm learning how to make healthy choices like those supermoms I see on T.V.

We spend hours on the trails behind our house, walking Tempest. Free from the distraction of video games and the kitchen table that still isn't put together, we talk. On miles of paved walkways that follow an old railroad corridor, beneath a canopy of trees, I get to know my son for the first time.

In the years that I was chasing dope, he was growing up. No longer a baby and not quite a teenager, he lives within that gap between innocence and experience. He still believes in Santa, but I also know that my sudden absence from his life created insecurities, and he has questions.

"Mom, why did you do drugs?" he asks me during one of our walks.

I am unprepared for the question—moments ago, we were talking about Megatron and Optimus Prime. I have known that there would eventually be a talk between us about my addiction, but I always expected that I would be the one to initiate it.

Daniel had made me aware of how he had handled Mason's questions over the years and the information he had shared with him. In the early days, he was told, "Mommy is sick, and she is in the hospital." As he got older, Daniel knew that he couldn't protect Mason from the harsh realities of my addiction forever. Still, he made sure that any information that he gave would in no way affect any possible future relationship between Mason and me.

I can never say it enough: Daniel is a good man, an incredible father, and I know that I am lucky.

"I made a terrible choice," I say, stopping and turning toward my son. "One that I will always wish I could take back." I struggle to find the right words, wanting to get this right. "My mistake hurt you, and I'm sorry about that. From the bottom of my heart, I'm sorry. Mason, I love you more than anything in the world, and I promise I will never do drugs again." I feel the tears falling down my face.

"It's okay, Mom," he says in the uncomplicated way that only children can do. I forgive you." Turning away, he grabs Tempests' leash from my hands. "I love you too," he declares before walking down the trail and heading towards home.

Despite everything I have done and all the hurt I've caused, he still loves me. Children are quick to forgive the things that we, as parents, have a hard time forgiving in ourselves. As I stare after him, I can feel the fracture in my heart start to heal and know that as long as I stay clean, everything will be ok.

9

TEST OF WILLS

Dear Cage,

Are you mad at me for some reason? Since I left Texas, I haven't heard from you. Maybe you didn't get my last letter with my new address, but please write me back.

Things in Kentucky are fantastic! I've been able to keep Mason every night since I moved into the new place. My mom was here for a while but left a few weeks ago. I miss her, but Mason is keeping me busy! I feel like a total mom — I take him to school and pick him up every day. Still working on learning to cook, but he likes Mac and Cheese the best anyway, so I'm getting by. I'm so in love with my kid.

The new house is chaos, boxes and

furniture are everywhere, but it's slowly coming together. I can't wait for you to see it! There is a seven-mile nature trail that starts literally out my front door. A beautiful stream runs beside it, with a rocky grotto beneath a bridge, and horse farms for as far as the eye can see. It's peaceful, and I'm happy here.

And it's a lot easier to stay clean here; I don't know anybody or have any triggers. I know I could get dope if I wanted it, but as the days pass, I find that I think of it less and less. This is the way life is supposed to be, and I think my body is starting to remember that.

I've been going to Masons soccer games, even bought myself a cute little chair to sit on. At first, I was nervous about going. I'm sure that the other parents have wondered about Mason's mom all these years, and suddenly I show up. But everybody has been so kind. I don't understand how the game is played and probably cheer for the wrong team sometimes, but it's been fun!

I miss you and think about you all the time. As I unpack boxes, there are so many memories. I get lost in daydreams, remembering us together and the life we used to have—the life before dope. I love you, Cage.

Love,
  Wind

"Are you going to be okay?"

Glancing through the open window of my car, I stare up at Daniel and watch as concern plays across his face. Forcing a fake smile on my face, I say, "Of course! It will be nice to have a break from the spawn for a few days." Despite my smile, I didn't mean it.

After months of being with Mason and my mom, tonight would be the first time I would be entirely on my own since I had gotten clean. I would be lying if I didn't say that I was a little scared, but I owed it to Daniel to reassure him. He had let me keep Mason every day since I had moved here, and it wasn't because he was the one who wanted a break, though I know he deserved one. No, he had let me keep him because he knew that I would struggle with being alone, and he worried that I might relapse. He wanted Mason to have his mom back more than anything, and he was willing to do whatever he could to help me.

"Well, you know you can call me if you need anything."

"I know. I still have a million boxes to unpack. I will be fine!" I smile convincingly up at him. "I promise, Daniel!" Nodding his head, he walks to the front of the car where Mason is waiting impatiently. "I love you, kiddo," I call out the window.

"Love you too, Mom." I watch through the windshield as Daniel, his hand resting on Mason's back, leads him up the walkway and disappears into the house. My heart constricts; I miss him already. As hard as the last few weeks have been, there was comfort in the routine we had developed—a sort of rhythm that beat through the days and rolled across the nights. Our little bubble felt safe, tucked away, and secure. Without Mason, I suddenly feel hollow and hesitant, not sure of what I should do next. Except back out of Daniel's driveway before I make it weird.

Heading for home, I resolve to finally tackle the chore I've been dreading and get the stupid kitchen table put together. I have been putting it off since the day we unloaded the moving truck. I knew it would suck, but if I kept procrastinating, I would turn into a real hoarder—shaming my mother even more.

Twenty minutes later, I stand in the open doorway of the garage, a sea of dusty boxes spread out before me, and try to pull together the courage to get started.

These containers have been sitting in storage for years, holding pieces of my past and the life I threw away. It was a miracle that they made it through my drug addiction at all. If it hadn't been for my mom paying my monthly storage bill, my memories and the history of my life would be sitting in a landfill somewhere, decomposing and buried. Forgotten, as if they had never existed at all.

Okay, I'm probably being a little dramatic, especially considering that there are more than a few cartons that have the word "Christmas" scrolled across them. We all know those boxes. The ones full of tangled lights, smashed bows, and the stocking you've had since you were six years old.

I see a box labeled "Other" and immediately elect to put that one off until the very end, knowing it was one of those boxes where random shit went to die.

Sitting cross-legged on the concrete floor, I decide just to dive right in, starting with the box of high school yearbooks. Lugging out the one from my senior year, I run my fingers over the blue and gold cover and read the words printed proudly across the top: "Clovis High School, Class of 1996." It makes me feel old as hell. Thumbing through the pages, I turn to my picture and have to laugh at how terrible I looked. For the love of God, why didn't anybody tell me that I looked appalling with white-blonde hair and a perm? How were perms ever even a thing? Like, damn, I looked better when I was banging dope every day. Shuddering, I return the book to the box and determine that it would probably be better for my mental health if I never looked at that photo again.

Shifting my body, I turn to the left and see the words "misc tech" scrawled across the side of a white carton. I don't need to open it to know what's inside: every type of cable that had ever been manufactured. Ethernet cables, HDMI cords, VGA cables, SATA ports, and the entire family of USB cables—it was the classic tweaker box. Everybody on meth has one. Everybody I knew, at least. I honestly don't know why we collected them. The electronics these cords connected to were sold to a pawn shop or traded for dope long ago. Of course, I do recall the many hours I spent untangling and lovingly organizing them.

I grab the box before I can change my mind and walk straight to the dumpster at the end of the ally. I hesitate briefly as I lift the carton above my head, worrying that I might actually need a thirty-pin iPhone connector one day. I quickly shake the thought out of my head; it's been six years since Apple made phones that need one. I push the box over the side, listen as it hits the bottom of the can with a thud, and head back to the garage, feeling proud of myself.

I pull open a blue plastic container, and my heart catches

when I see that it is full of Mason's baby stuff. Smiling, I reach down and rub my hands over the blanket in which we brought him home from the hospital. Remembering how I had freaked out on Daniel about not driving too fast, I chuckle. He had responded with, "Honey, this is Los Angeles, and we're going to be stuck in traffic all the way home. Calm down."

I pull out the books that I read to him before he could even talk, his first pair of Nikes from his dad, and the little glass jar that holds his first lost tooth. I haul out stacks of baby clothes and bring them to my face, inhaling deeply, trying to capture the baby smell that has long since faded away.

I am suddenly so grateful that my mom had the forethought to pay the bill for my storage directly instead of giving me cash to pay for it myself, knowing that I would use the money to buy dope. And she would have been right, and my addiction would have taken these boxes of memories away from me too.

Over the next few hours, I take a trip down memory lane, every box full of surprises and sentimental stuff that I hadn't thought about in years. I enjoy this, despite how dirty I'm getting, and grab a green plastic storage crate.

Peering down at the contents, I already know that this is a random shit kind of box—tubes of glitter that had long since dried up, craft scissors, half-melted candles, a stapler with no staples, and reams of brightly-colored construction paper—all items from my failed arts and crafts stage. I start sorting it all into piles. My "garbage" pile is growing satisfyingly larger than my "keep" pile.

I've emptied half of the bin when I catch a glimpse of something from the corner of my eye that makes me stop. Frozen, I focus my gaze towards the back of the box, and my mouth goes dry. I feel my heart race, heat flooding my face and across the back of my neck.

No. Freaking. Way.

Half-buried beneath a pack of index cards and a piece of ripped blue tissue paper, tucked into the corner, is the past I left behind. My serenity completely gone, I stare intently as the colors come together in my head—orange, green, white—and collide with memories that I've been trying so hard to forget.

Holy shit.

I reach into the box and pinch the edge of the exposed plastic. With my heart slamming in my chest, I free it from its casket and bring it to my face. Dangling in front of my nose is a full, unopened bag of insulin syringes—rigs, pins, hypos—the toxic partner to dope; my kit.

Over the years, my storage unit became much more than just a big metal box that held the residue of my life before addiction. It was also where I would live when I had nowhere else to go, a place to hide when I wanted to be alone, and most importantly, it's where I would spend hours of my life getting high.

I don't know why I'm shocked to see the needles or feel offended by their presence. I used to hide bags of them everywhere, making sure I had clean points whenever I needed them. The silence around me feels heavy, and the sudden solitude makes it easy to slip into the one place I shouldn't go alone—my head.

Naturally, discovering a stash of hidden rigs leads right to another thought: what else had I hidden in these boxes? What other treasures had I squirreled away and forgotten about? Is it possible that somewhere in this profusion of cardboard boxes and plastic containers, I had entombed the most expensive commodity I had ever owned? The one that once cost me far more than all my money and assets—it had cost me, my soul. I traded *everything* that I loved for that *one* thing.

Crystal meth.

On the surface, it looks innocuous enough—like broken shards of glass or slivers of crushed ice. I would often compare it to the rock candy my parents used to buy me at Disneyland when I was a kid. But instead of sugary blocks of sweetness on a stick, the crystals are sold in tiny plastic bags. Small packets that contain the portal to hell and a bottomless pit of torment.

Tucking my newly-found prize into the bra strap on my shoulder, I grab the container still open in front of me and tip it over, spilling the contents all over the floor. I drop to my hands and knees and pick through the mess, examining and tossing aside every jar, paper clip, and takeout menu. I run my hands along every side and corner of the box, feeling for a piece of taped plastic.

Moving onto the next unopened box, I rip it open and ransack the insides. I pull out old clothes and search through every pocket and scrutinize every fold of the fabric. I remove the battery compartment for every flashlight and shake them until they are empty.

Manic now, I rip apart boxes, desperation hurling me forward. In a frenzy, I claw through the piles on the ground, hunting for the dope that must be hidden somewhere in this chaotic mess. I break apart Mason's old toys looking for forgotten hiding spots and destroy memory boxes filled with the things I had stored away to keep forever. I am completely consumed with the battle inside my head.

Finding half of my kit is like a cruel joke. I need its playmate; its other half. I need both parts because I need to get high. All thoughts of my kid, my new life, and second chance, every promise I had made to my mom, and every vow I had whispered to myself are forgotten.

I find nothing.

Maybe it's luck or a gift from God, but I don't feel grateful. The only things I feel are disappointment and overwhelming frustration. Sitting in the middle of the garage, surrounded by piles of trash and pieces of my life, I bury my face in my hands and cry.

As the sobs roll through me, shaking my body, I hear a comforting sound—the rustle of plastic, my other gift, this one from Satan.

What did I love nearly as much as meth? The ritual. This part of the experience was once as intoxicating as actually being high. I may not have dope or a way to get any, but I do have a pretty good consolation prize: a full bag of syringes.

Springing up, I leap across the mountains of junk like a game of Frogger and run through my back door into my house. Grabbing a bottle of water from the counter, I cross to my living room. I twist off the top and lower myself onto the brand new couch that my mom had just bought me.

Ripping open the bag, I pull out a rig. I can feel my heartbeat pulse in my throat. I slide my hand down the transparent cylinder, letting my eyes scan the bold black numbers and thin lines. The orange cap feels familiar between my fingers, the sensation intimate.

I can already anticipate the pain of the needle sliding into my skin, sharp and gratifying. My mouth waters as I imagine hitting my mark, the elusive vein that can't hide forever, and envisioning the blood as it shoots back into the rig makes my heart race.

I remove the cap, and a popping sound fills the silent room. The sudden contrast makes me hesitate, leaving room for a conversation inside my head.

You need to do this to get it out of your system. You can do it once and never do it again. It's not a big deal—it's not like you're about to bang dope. It's only water.

A cold finger of doubt slips between my ribs and rubs across my soul.

Will shooting up with water be considered a relapse, though? Will I lose my clean time and have to start over?

I'm stuck in this test of resolve within my mind, locked in a stalemate with myself.

Who would even know?

Nobody.

But I would know.

I hear a thud above my head, followed by the sounds of my dog barreling down the stairs. Tempest comes into the room and stares at me with eyes the same color as my own—amber brown and flecked with gold veins. She could be my twin if not for the whole "different species" thing.

Honestly, I was never a dog person. Or an animal person at all, really. Selfish and preferring to have as little responsibilities for others as possible, I never wanted pets. Having a kid was way more work than I thought it would be, but at least they didn't shit on the floor. Not usually, anyway. So, my desire to get a dog had nothing to do with forming a bond with a creature that had a lot more chromosomes than I did and everything to do with feeling safe—and not being alone.

The dope game isn't a safe place to be, especially for a woman. I quickly learned that security wouldn't be found in a man, especially not men that were chasing dope. So, I decided to get a dog, the scariest one I could find.

From the moment I saw her picture on Craigslist, I knew that Tempest was born for me. And I know that having her not only protected me during situations that could have otherwise turned violent but also saved my life in the moments when I wanted to die.

She was with me, always, the most constant thing in my life. She kept me warm during the cold nights we slept in the car. She never left my side during the hours I laid on the bathroom floor, trying to find a vein. I took her to trap houses and cried into her fur whenever I felt the grief of being away from Mason. She forgave me for suspecting she worked for the FBI when I was paranoid from several sleepless days of slamming dope. Tempest was my best friend and one of my many reasons for wanting to get clean. She deserved a better life than I was giving her. And she was sick of McDonald's cheeseburgers.

I watch her walk toward me, her beautiful Doberman face searching mine. I know that she can feel my distress; she always can. Stopping beside me, Tempest leans against my legs and pushes her head against my thigh. The weight of her body is enough to quiet the voices in my head. I drop the needle onto the table and lean down to kiss the top of her back, grateful for this amazing animal.

Feeling empowered for not giving in, I sweep the loose needle and bag of rigs into my hand and carry them over to my garbage can, dropping them in. Even though the trash bag is only half-full, I decide to get rid of it.

I peek out the door and glance both ways to make sure nobody is outside. I don't know why, but I'm worried that if somebody sees me, they might wonder what's in the bag. Or know about what I had almost done to myself.

I quickly walk to the dumpster, toss the bag over the side, and book it back to the safety of my house.

The pride I felt for making the right choice has already ebbed away. I feel empty, a colossal void growing inside me. I hate it. I just want to feel better or feel something that makes me happy. I don't want to get high or do anything that will hurt my family, but I want to do *something*.

I'm kid-free, mom-free, and don't have anybody around to tell me what to do. Suddenly, the answer comes to me, and I know exactly what I need.

I need to get laid.

10

CHURCH BASEMENTS

Rushing back into the house, I jump in the shower and blast the hot water. I lean against the wall and scrub myself down with soap. The syrupy smells of sweet pea, pear, and freesia envelop me, and I take my time, enjoying the ritual of being a woman.

When the water starts to get cold, I pull myself out and wrap my body in a thick, fluffy towel. I twist another one up into my hair. Using my hand to wipe the steam from the mirror, I stare at my face and do my best not to notice how round my cheeks have gotten. The recovery weight is piling on, and I feel helpless to stop it. Starting tomorrow, I'm going on a diet. I ignore the fact that I have been saying this pretty much every day since I had gotten clean.

Pushing the negative vibes out of my mind, I head to the closet to get dressed. Tempest, my constant shadow, is sprawled out across the bed, fast asleep. She is going to hate it when I come home tonight, and she realizes that I'm not alone. She isn't a fan of men, especially the ones that she has to share me with.

I pull on a black thong that is a little too snug before struggling into my favorite pair of jeans. I have to wriggle around to get them over my ass and nearly cry when I have to suck my breath in to close the button. My fat rolls up into the dreaded muffin top, and I try to conceal it by pulling the waistband higher. This, in turn, makes the seam of my pants is ride into the center of my vagina, giving me a camel toe. *Damnit.*

I'm contemplating the safety of using a butter knife and vacuum cleaner to perform emergency liposuction when I hear my phone vibrate.

"Who the hell is calling me?" I ask Tempest as I pass her. Her left eye squints at me, but she doesn't answer. Rude.

I grab the phone from where I left it on the bathroom counter and glance at the number. No contact, but I feel a rush of excitement when I recognize the Texas area code. I wait impatiently while the automated system leads me through the prompts. I agree to pay the insane amount of money that the prison system charges for phone calls—calls that cost nothing in the free world—before they connect us. A few beeps later, I hear the static clear, and the line between us is open.

I can hear the love in his voice when he says my name. "Wind."

"Hey, baby, I'm so glad you called. I've been missing you like crazy," I say truthfully, but feel a smidge of guilt moving through me. I do miss Cage—a lot. But I also realize that starting my life over here in Kentucky is much easier and less complicated without balancing Mason's needs and an obsession with my ex.

"I miss you too. Are you staying clean?"

"Yes sir," I reply proudly. "Every day, all day long."

"Good. How's Mason? Is he glad to have his mom back?"

"He is so great, and of course he loves having me back. I spoil the shit out of him," I add, laughing.

"You always did spoil him. You're lucky he hasn't turned into a brat," he says jokingly.

"You used to spoil him too. Actually, I just unpacked that fancy skateboard you got him. Remember? It was our first Christmas together."

I smile as the memory pulls me back—our little family, sitting on the floor in front of the Christmas tree. Cage and I were blurry-eyed from waking up so early, but not Mason. He had been racing around, shaking the gifts, and checking to see if Santa had eaten the cookies we'd left out. After confirming that three cookies were missing, courtesy of Cage, he wanted to know how Santa had gotten into the house to leave gifts—we didn't have a chimney.

"He has a magic key that he uses to come through the front door," Cage explained. "I don't think he comes down chimneys anymore anyway. He's too fat."

Mason giggled, crawled into my lap, and leaned back against me. Cage handed him a big box wrapped in bright red paper covered in white snowmen and said, "This one is for you from your mom and me."

Settled in my lap, Mason tore the box apart. Inside was the black and blue skateboard Cage had bought him. And he immediately wanted to go outside and ride it.

"Not yet, kiddo," I told him. "You need a helmet first."

Rolling his eyes, Cage scooped Mason out of my arms, grabbed the skateboard, and headed outside. Smiling after them, I felt content. I was happy.

My heart constricts when I remember that was the last time we had been together. Not long after, our journey into madness had started, and our world had fallen apart.

Breaking into my thoughts, Cage whispers, "I remember." I can hear the regret in his voice. "So, how do you like Kentucky?"

"I love it! It's not as exciting as Dallas, but it is gorgeous here," I gush before I can stop myself. Damnit, why did I have to bring up Dallas? I know better than that.

I can feel the shift in his mood before he even says a word. It's going to be all downhill from here, and I have nobody to blame but myself.

"Missing the big D, huh?" Cage says, and I can tell from his voice that he's sneering.

I know that he isn't talking about the city, but I try to divert the conversation before it goes sideways. "Babe," I say, pausing for the space of a heartbeat, "I don't miss Dallas at all. I'm really happy here."

"Amanda, I'm glad you're happy. I just figured you were missing all your men in Texas."

He might as well have just reached over and slapped me across the face. Would there ever come a time that Cage would forgive me for who I had become on dope? We had both screwed up, and while it was horrific, it was also understandable. On meth, we became different people.

"Cage, please stop," I beg.

"Do you have any idea how many nights I've laid awake imagining all the men that were screwing you? That you were spreading your legs for? How many times did you bang like a whore to get dope?" Disgust and hate drip off of his words, into my mouth, and slides into my heart.

"You're wrong. It wasn't like that!"

Well, it hadn't *exactly* been like that, anyway. I had slept with guys I would never have looked twice at if I hadn't been using drugs—gross men that I push out of my head whenever their faces appear, embarrassed for myself. But there had never been a time where I was given money or dope in exchange for sex. I just banged for free, and I guess that might even be worse.

"Look, I will tell you anything you want to know and be completely honest. Just talk to me," I plead. "I feel like you are making things up in your head—things that are worse than what really happened."

Cage's voice is thick with bitterness. "Do you know why I broke up with you when I started using again? It was because I knew that meth would turn you into a whore, and it did. That's all you are now."

Cage has always been a master at delivering emotional pain. He knows exactly where to slide the blade so that it cuts the deepest. The woman I used to be, the one before dope, would be crying by now, broken by his words. Probably lying at his feet, apologizing for whatever he thought I had done wrong. The woman I became on meth could be just as evil as he was, and if we were having this conversation when I was still getting high, I would probably tell him how much I had loved screwing his favorite drug dealer. And his dealer's girlfriend.

Now, I was neither of those women.

"I'm not going to sit here and let you talk to me like this. Write to me or call back when you've calmed down. I love you, Cage." I hang up, sighing with relief.

Built from red brick and stone, the church was ancient. Walking through the arched and column-lined doorway, I step into the vestibule. It smells like dying flowers, frankincense, and Pine-Sol, reminding me of my grandma's house.

A few are people walking down a side hallway, and I quickly follow them. They must be headed to the same place as me; who else would be at church on Friday night except for a bunch of addicts? At the end of the corridor, I make a left and walk into an empty room. I look around and can't figure out where everybody has gone. I don't see any doors or hallways except for the one I just came down. It's like they just disappeared. It's creepy, and I think it's time for me to leave.

I'm about to turn around and haul ass when I hear a sound coming from the opposite side of the room. Tucked into a little nook that has been built into the corner of the wall, I watch as a door opens and a man comes out. Before I can find my voice and ask him for directions, he walks past me, smelling like stale cigarettes, and I listen to his footsteps disappear behind me.

I scurry across the gleaming white marble floors to the door and pull it open. A small landing leads to a staircase that spirals down into the darkness. Of course. Twelve-step meetings are always held in the basement.

Standing there, I contemplate the wisdom of taking the first step; this is how people get murdered in the movies. But I also remember hearing in a meeting back home that you won't stay clean if you don't take that first step. So, down I go, praying to God that Michael Myers isn't waiting for me.

When I reach the bottom, I walk around the wooden newel post into a dimly-lit room. A few dozen metal folding chairs are set up in rows with maybe fifteen people sitting in them. I sit down in one at the back, disappointed that I can't see anybody's faces.

I came here under the guise of getting spiritual, but really, I came to find a guy to bang. And based on the rear-view of heads I'm seeing, I'll be having sex with myself tonight.

I'm doing this recovery shit all wrong. On the other hand, I rationalize, having sex isn't the same as relapsing on dope. I mean, I probably wouldn't head on down to an old building in the city to steal copper wire to trade for dick.

Still, deep down, even if you removed the drug addiction, my biggest problem has always been love. And for my entire adult life, I have used sex to feel it. I don't know why I am the way I am, but I suspect it might have something to do with what happened to me in the orange orchard behind my parent's house when I was six years old. My rehab doctor recommended that I get into therapy to deal with my childhood issues, and I know she was right, but I'm not ready to deal with the things that I've buried so deeply.

The call from Cage had gotten to me. I know he wasn't right. Not completely anyway. When I was strung out on meth, my behavior could in no way be compared to any other time in my life. Especially now. Like, I haven't had sex in forever. Well, at least a few months.

Even beyond my need to make myself feel better with sex, I'm struggling to figure out who I am as a person now. Once I got clean, I thought I would feel like the woman I was before the addiction, but I don't. I feel like an observer in my own life, not participating, just watching. Sometimes it's like I'm trapped in prison, one that's been created from my sins. I'm screaming for help, but no sound comes out.

Suddenly, I want to be anywhere other than the basement of this musty church. Standing up, I trace my way back through the route I had come. Crossing the deserted street, the gutter lined with trash, I walk to my car and climb inside.

A bank of fog is spilling across the road, and I shiver with cold while I stare out the windshield, trying to decide what I'm going to do now. Kentucky no longer seems all that beautiful, warm, or

Addict Chick unCaged

welcoming. And the realization that I'm here alone, with no friends to call or family to see, makes me ache.

The long night stretching out in front of me, I slide the car into drive and take off with no destination in mind. I'm not even sure how to get back home without the help of GPS.

I had expected that it would be easy to find somebody to take home; it always had been before. At least, it had been when I was getting high. I consider going to a bar, but that has never been my thing. Besides, it looks like all the bars that I pass are filled with college kids from the nearby campus, and young guys have also never been my thing.

I feel empty inside, and I'm desperate to fill the void with something. Something that isn't meth, and apparently, it wasn't going to be a dick either. Feeling defeated, I search my GPS for the only thing that might make me feel better—Chick-fil-A, the best fast food establishment ever created—and head that way.

Thirty minutes later, I roll through my front door with a half-empty strawberry shake, a headache, and no regrets. Tempest comes crashing down the stairs to greet me and licks at the Chick-fil-A sauce that had dribbled down the front of my shirt.

Grabbing a bottle of ibuprofen out of the cabinet, I struggle to get the stupid childproof cap off. Finally, I rip it apart and spill green gel caps everywhere.

"Damnit," I moan, dropping to my knees and sweeping them into my hand. Dusting the dirt off, I toss a few into my mouth and take a swig from my shake to wash them down.

Plopping down on the couch, I lean back into the cushions and pull out my phone. I don't have a T.V. to entertain me yet, so I pull up Facebook and start scrolling. My relationship with the social media platform is relatively new. When it first became popular, I barely used it. I was too busy being a mom and working my ass off at my job. I think I might have signed up for the app when I got the first iPhone in 2007, but I still didn't understand why anybody would want to put their business out there like that. Plus, I hated how I looked and wasn't about to announce my crippling insecurities all over cyberspace.

That all changed when I began my sojourn into the dope game. Meth has the uncanny ability to make you feel like you're the hottest chick in the world—alluring and untouchable. It was the first and only time in my life that I felt pretty or desirable. Going from a size fourteen to a size three will do that for you. I made the standard and extremely embarrassing mistake that most people on meth do: I started posting pictures all over Facebook, thinking that nobody would know that I was strung out.

They did.

I mean, how could they not? I posted pictures of my butt in booty shorts, no words or explanation, just a full-on photo of my half-naked ass. I shared pictures wearing only a bra and thong, standing in the middle of a pile of trash. There was no limit to how far I went with the images that I splashed across social media. My mom was horrified and unfriended me.

After I got clean, I wanted to die when I saw the evidence of my craziness. I purged my profile, disgusted with myself and mortified by what I had done. I didn't look pretty at all; I looked sick.

Shuddering at the memory, I flick my finger over the screen to refresh the feed. A random image pops up, and my gaze is immediately drawn to it. Standing against a white background is a dark-haired girl covered in tattoos. She kind of reminds me of myself before I gorged on Chick-fil-A. There is a filter over the picture, making it appear gray. A quote, written in dark red, is scrolled across the front. *Drugs take you to hell disguised as heaven.*

Oh, that's good stuff. I quickly save the image to my phone. Going back to the post, I try to figure out who had made the quote on my friend's list. The name written in bold black says, "Keep the plug in the jug." I don't have a friend with that name, so this confuses me. I click on the words, and I'm directed to a new profile. It looks different than any I've ever seen. In the middle of the page, to the far right, is a thumbs-up sign. My finger hovers over the icon for a moment, and it turns blue when I click it.

I click on the tab for photos and am shocked when I see hundreds—no, thousands—of these little quotes, most of which are about addiction and recovery. As I scan, I realize that I can relate to nearly all of them. It's like everything that I've gone through and everything that I'm feeling is right here in these words. I quickly get sucked in and start saving them onto my phone.

I wonder if this kind of thing is even allowed in our twelve-step program. Haven't I learned in my meetings that anonymity is the spiritual foundation or something like that? I'm not really sure how it all works, except that it doesn't seem like we're supposed to talk about addiction outside of meetings. I could be totally wrong—I don't have a sponsor yet, and I think they are the ones that tell you the rules and shit.

I still don't understand what I'm looking at, so I scroll back up to the top and see that forty-five thousand people have liked this profile. This obviously isn't a typical profile because Facebook only allows a maximum of five thousand friends. In real life, I have maybe five. I find it interesting that so many people have liked "Keep the plug in the jug" because that seems like a lot of drug addicts to me.

I close out of Facebook and press the notebook icon on my phone screen and get lost in thought while I wait for it to open.

When I entered treatment, I was an emotional wreck. My rehab doctor said that it was common to be overwhelmed and suggested that I keep a journal. I balked because written evidence of my sickness was the last thing I wanted to have. Ideally, I would forget about this chaotic chapter in my life and move on.

I have always loved to write, but this was different because I would be writing about myself, not some fictional character. Doc assured me that there was no right or wrong way to journal and said that pouring myself out of my head and onto paper would help me see things in a more objectable way. She reasoned that it would be a way for me to dig deep and healthily connect with my emotions. I wasn't sure about all that, but it did make me feel better. Sometimes I wrote lines and lines of scattered thoughts, and sometimes I would just jot down a few sentences or words.

I scan through all the journal entries I've written, my most shameful secrets, and wonder if I would have the courage to share any of it. Would it shock people to know that I struggled with a drug addiction? Everybody that I care about already knows, so what would my motivation be to talk about it publicly?

Am I ashamed of being a drug addict? No, but I am embarrassed about the person I became when I was high. I have paralyzing guilt for the pain I caused my family, and regret over the life I threw away will live inside me forever. I'm deeply ashamed of many things, but struggling with substance abuse isn't one of them.

I mean, I do have some good quotes of my own—almost as good as those on that Jug page. However, I have no idea how they had gotten the words on top of the pictures.

Making a quick decision, I open the Facebook app and go to my profile. Clicking on the icon to upload a picture, I select one of the ones I downloaded from the Jug page. It reads, "I am a proudly recovering drug addict." I take a moment to crop the name off of the bottom so that people will think I made it, then upload the picture.

I stare at the space above the stolen quote and gather my thoughts. What should I write? Am I prepared to put myself on blast and own my truth? What would people think? Maybe being honest and sharing my story might reach somebody who's struggling. Writing has been cathartic for me, but am I ready to share my secrets with my entire friend's list?

I begin writing.

```
I have a confession to make. Most of you
probably already know, but for those of
you that don't, I have struggled with an
addiction to meth for the last four years.
I entered treatment on February 4th, 2015,
and have been clean ever since. I'm not
sure why I decided to share this; I know
that the topic of addiction is taboo, but
for some crazy reason, writing about it
has helped me stay clean. At least,
so far.
```

Before I can chicken out, I post the confession and send my greatest shame out onto the internet for all to read. Opening myself up like that feels good, and I have this burning desire to keep writing, wanting to pour myself onto paper. Or onto my old laptop, at least.

I grab the device off the table and pull it into my lap. Opening the word processor, I stare at the blank screen and figure out where to start. The wide-open space on my computer feels much more daunting than the narrow spot on my phone. There was a lot of room for words that I suddenly couldn't find.

Cage's face flashes into my head. It was unsettling how just the thought of him could snap me out of the present and drag me back into the past. However, I now know exactly what I want to write: I want to go back to the beginning, the moment I met Cage. It's like my entire life began that day, and I want to go back and remember. I want him to remember. And I want him to know the truth. I want him to know how much I love him, despite the mistakes we both made.

I'll write our story, every part. I will begin from the first night we met and our first concert together, from our first night in bed to all the nights in between. I want to go back to the minute we fell in love and remember how my body responded to his touch and mouth. I need him to know how he made me feel every second that we were together.

I start to write, and the words just flow. I fill page after page with the story of our lives. I don't worry about form, syntax, or grammar; I only stream the memories in my head through the tips of my fingers onto the keyboard. I plan to go back and clean it up before I print it out and send it to Cage.

Writing about all the good memories with Cage is easy; reliving our incredible sex is even easier. The only time there is a pause in the pounding of the keys is when I remember something else, a moment I had forgotten, and have to go back and include those details. But then I get to the part of the story that changed everything, and I stop typing.

Sitting up straight, I stare into space and let the memory wash over me, bringing with it the most terrifying moment of my life. Inside my head, I can hear the echo of my scream and the horror and panic I felt that day. It slices into me, making me bleed.

The day I found Cage with a needle in his arm, and I thought he was dead. The day our love story ended and our nightmare began.

I consider just ending there. I could type "The End" at the bottom of the last page, close my laptop, and call it a night. I could protect myself from things I don't want to remember and just go to sleep.

But it wasn't the end, was it? The day that Cage relapsed on heroin was just the end of the beginning. Even at this very second, our book doesn't have a conclusion. How can I tell our story without including all the moments between then and now? Simple: I can't. That would be like reading the first half of a book, closing it, and never knowing what happens at the end.

I want Cage to know the truth, even if that means I will never have his forgiveness. And maybe somewhere within these pages, I might be able to find forgiveness for myself.

I write through the entire night.

I go back to the day I first got high with Cage, and the moment I decided that sliding a needle of dope into my arm was the right thing to do. I comb through my memory, wondering what had been so broken in my soul that I had felt like it was the only choice I had. Was it my deeply rooted need for love, the kind that superseded even the love I had for Cage?

So many questions float through my mind, and I have very few answers. This emotional drive down memory lane has been draining, and I can no longer process anything. So, I close my eyes and lay down on the couch. With my body pressed behind Tempest, I throw my arm over her and let sleep pull me into the darkness

11

THE LITTLE BOOK OF ADDICT CHICK

The next morning, my body feels like it has been run over by a truck. My dog is asleep across my legs, my head is at an odd angle, and I'm pretty sure my boob has fallen out of the side of my tank top. I crack open my eyes and wince at the sunlight filtering through the blinds. Rubbing my fingers over my face, I feel that gross shit that accumulates when you sleep and wonder what time it is.

I disentangle Tempest from my legs and watch as she jumps off the couch and clambers upstairs. The little bitch is going back to bed. Rolling over onto my side, I reach for my phone and bring it to my face. Alerts are scrolling up the screen—fast.

"Oh. My. God!" I screech as I realize that the notifications are all coming from Facebook.

Also, I'm mortified to see that my boob had indeed escaped from my tank and is still hanging out there. Tucking the girl back where she belongs, I turn my attention back to my phone. Scared even to look, certain that I have been crucified over my post from last night, I touch one of the notifications. With trepidation, I watch as it automatically opens the Facebook app and drops me into the comments section.

```
Congrats, I am so proud of you!

We are praying for you and love you so
much!

I think it's great that you're sharing
your story!

Thanks for the inspiration!

I'm a gratefully recovering addict too!
```

There are at least a few hundred comments. I get a rush of adrenaline as I read all the encouraging words and realize that I love this shit. A flame lights inside my chest, and I immediately decide to share more of my recovery journey. Obviously, people want to hear about it, and all of the positive comments make me feel good. I haven't felt motivated by anything in forever and now I feel like I might have found my purpose.

I need to figure out how to make a profile like "Keep the plug in the jug." After a quick Google search, I learn about something called Facebook Pages and set about making one of my own. The very first question slows my roll. Facebook wants to know what the name of my page will be. I have no idea so I toss ideas around in my head. The Junkie Journal? The Addict Diary? The Adventures of a Recovering Addict? I can't believe how difficult this is. I run to the kitchen and grab a pen and notebook; I needed to see the words on paper. Facebook makes it clear that changes in names would be considered but not guaranteed. I don't want to screw this up.

I scribble ideas as I think of them. The Recovering Junkie? The Addict in Recovery? Girl in Recovery? No, I don't like the ring of any of those.

What about The Drug Addict? Mulling it over, I don't love that one either. Besides, while I am—or rather, was—most definitely a drug addict, aren't I also a love addict? And a sex addict? Let's not forget my obsession with food. I'm pretty sure that I dance with the demon of gambling as well. Shaking my head, I push the memory of my scratcher addiction from my mind.

And then it comes to me, like an epiphany. I know what I can name my page: Addict Woman. That's exactly what I am, right? Hell, aren't most people addicted to at least one thing? Aside from the standard drug addiction, there are many behavioral addictions that people struggle with; shopping, video games, and the internet —I even saw a show that discussed an addiction to drinking urine. Like, human piss. Can you imagine? I felt better about my dope habit after seeing that program.

I write my idea down and study it. I'm not sure how I feel about the accidental play on the character Wonder Woman. No, I wanted something a little sexier and bolder than that. I do a quick Google search for synonyms of "woman" and scan the first article, reviewing my options.

Girl (not for a long time), wife (not anymore), lady (nope), virgin (definitely not), slave (what the hell?). My eye lands on the word "chick" and I write it down.

I practice putting words together and listen as they roll off my tongue. I stretch them out and emphasize each syllable. It feels right, and I know it's perfect.

I complete the sign-up process to create my new Facebook business page. I'm not prepared to call it a Fan page because that sounds egotistical, but I can't wait to get started. I'm on fire for something for the first time in longer than I can remember. Probably since before the addiction. I have direction and focus, and I have a feeling that I'm going to create something special.

Looking down at my newly-born page, I feel a charge course through me when I see the name at the top. "Addict Chick," I say, smiling, and send the words floating out into the world.

Creating a Facebook page was easy, but filling it with content has proven to be much harder. I have a lot to learn, and I make a bunch of mistakes. Without meaning to, I piss off a few people within the online recovery community. They have a right to be mad—I basically stole their hard work and passed it off as my own. Mainly when it came to those little square quotes that I soon learn have a name: *memes*.

I had never heard that term before, and part of me thinks it's a joke. I do a little research and find out the word *meme* started in academia, not on Facebook. It originated in a book called *The Selfish Gene* in 1976 by author and biologist Richard Dawkins. Science has never been my best subject, but the basic concept is that in the same way genes replicate and transmit from one being to the next, so do cultural ideas. Of course, the internet hijacked the term, and now we use it to describe content that is spread across our digital world.

When I first start Addict Chick, I do what most newbies do: download the memes from existing recovery pages, crop out the names, add my watermark, and post it like I actually made that shit. I carry on that way for a while, growing my following with others' content and feeling proud of how fast my page was spreading—until I get a message in my inbox from the creator of "Keep the plug in the Jug."

It isn't a nice message. I mean, he straight-up burns my ass and hands it back to me, making it perfectly clear that what I've been doing is wrong and that stealing isn't a part of recovery. Devastated and embarrassed, I apologize and claim plausible deniability because I am brand new.

And then he shows me what recovery is all about. He teaches me how to make memes and shares free programs that I can use because I didn't have any money. He advises me on the ethics of growing a page and teaches me about the Facebook algorithm's complexity. He becomes my mentor and helps me build a solid foundation for my page.

Once I get the meme piece down, I discover that even the act of creating a quote from my thoughts is helpful to me. And journaling has become so cathartic for me that I realize I want to share more text-based content on my social platforms.

For a while, I agonize over how much of my addiction I want to share. In the end, I decide that I'm going all in. I want to be honest and real. The message I share needs to be authentic because drug addicts understand each other, even in silence. Except, now, I would be recovering out loud and very publicly. I truly believe that if writing my thoughts is healing for me, then reading them might help somebody else. I want the words I write to resonate with at least one other person.

It doesn't take long to realize that talking about my journey through a debilitating meth addiction isn't enough, because life is an assortment of moments piled on top of each other. That's what creates the story of who you are. The seasons of your life become the history of your life.

It's true for all of us. We are so much more than just the bad choices we make, and we shouldn't be defined by one terrible decision or even a series of terrible decisions—the record of how you got there and what you did after matters too.

My story is filled with broken pieces, terrible choices, and ugly truths, but it's also filled with a badass comeback, peace in my soul, and grace that saved my life. And I want to write about all of it.

A few weeks later, I call my mom.

"Mama," I say, "I want to write a book."

There's a short pause. "That's great," she says, then pauses again. "About what?"

"I want to write about my addiction and life. You know—my story. I have pages of journal entries, and I know that I can turn it into a real book."

I can hear the uncertainty in her voice. "I know you loved to write when you were in high school, but do you know how to write a book? Because I'm sure hiring a ghostwriter would cost a lot of money, and we can't afford to do that."

I rolled my eyes. "No, Mom, I'm going to write it myself. I don't need a ghostwriter."

"Well, I love you and will support anything you want to do, but don't forget the deal we have. You need to get a job in the next few months. I'm running out of money to support you."

I try not to get frustrated with her response, even though she's raining on my parade. She was right, of course; I do need to get a job. Now that I'm clean, I can really feel the pain of being broke. When I was on dope, it only hurt when I didn't have the funds to get high.

"I promise I'll start looking for a job while I write the book," I tell her.

After the call, I set out on my new adventure. I'm going to write a book—as soon as I figure out how. Learning how a book comes together and how to do it on your own proves to be far more complicated than I thought it would be. It takes a lot of research and tears but eventually, I work out the technical side.

But determining what would go inside the book—the actual story—is the real challenge. Internally, I wrestle with what to include and how to write it. Putting together my thoughts in a way that read like a story is grueling, possibly the most arduous process I have ever put myself through.

In the beginning, I'm driven by my need to write about my love for Cage. In my mind, my addiction was entirely justified by the fact that I had loved him so much that I chose to get high with him rather than live without him. If I could make Cage see that, he would forgive me for everything else that I had done.

Everything changes once I begin. I turn myself inside out and dive into parts of my head that I haven't acknowledged in years. I share my worst secrets, open up my life, and learn things about myself that change everything I'm becoming.

I will never again be the woman I was before dope, nor the one I became when I was using. Now, I'm becoming somebody that I can be proud of.

I am becoming Addict Chick, and she is a badass.

12

LONELY AF

Dear Cage,

 I hate how our last phone call ended, but it drives me crazy when you bring up the past. We are both clean now, and I still hope that we can move on from all this. I forgive you for everything you did. I wish that you would forgive me too.

 I have to tell you something, and I'm not sure if you will like it, but I hope you will understand. Remember how I told you that I've been journaling? Well, I'm writing a book about my addiction, and about our life. I've started accounts on social media and named my brand "Addict Chick." What do you think of the name? It's been pretty amazing to build this sort of community. Most of the people that follow me are women, and I'm making tons of new friends.

I think a lot of them can relate to my story. Every chick has that *one* guy that they will love forever. The way that I love you. Please call me or write me back. I miss you!

Love,

Wind

I thought I understood loneliness when I was on drugs, but the true loneliness would come when I got clean and actually had to feel it. Moving to Kentucky was the right thing to do, but I have never lived anywhere that wasn't near some part of my family. I miss my mom every day, and adjusting to a new life is often painful. There are moments that I can feel the tears building and my throat constricting, for no reason except that I am alone.

I've never experienced depression before, but the first few months in my new home have been brutal. Especially during the times that Mason goes with his dad and the only voices I hear are the ones inside my head. My emotions are all over the place, and when they hit me, they feel so real that they torment me in physical ways. I'm exhausted all day, but at night, I lay awake with a brain that won't shut down. And when sleep finally takes me, the nightmares are there, waiting. And they're terrifying.

The brain is arguably the most powerful organ in the human body. It produces our every action, feeling, memory, and experience in the world. And it has become a vault for my own personal hell. When I'm asleep and vulnerable, meth visits me, and he is relentless.

Behind my closed eyelids, the dark memories of my addiction play like a movie that was filmed in black and white with flashes of red. The vision of crimson blood shooting back into my needle and dripping down my arms is so vivid and feels so real that I can taste the dope when it hits the back of my throat, I can hear my cough when it finds my heart, and I can feel the throbbing between my legs while it races through my veins. The faces of the men I took to bed have Satan's eyes, and they float across my vision like I'm standing in the middle of a game of Fifty-Two Pick Up.

On the screen, I watch myself fill a syringe of water from the back of a filthy toilet, then sit down on a dirt floor littered with trash and smelling like death and decay. I stab holes into my body in the never-ending chase for a viable vein, mutilating my arms, legs, and even my feet. Blood pools around me, and flowing to the edge of my vision—drops into nothingness.

I hear Mason screaming for me and watch as he's ripped away and carried into the darkness, sobbing. The voice that beats in my thoughts demands that I get high, even if that means that my child is lost forever. The urgency to go to him is so powerful that I can feel it rise within me and explode from my soul.

I wake up screaming, covered in sweat, and desperate to separate my dreams from reality. I slap myself across the face in an attempt to shake free from the trail of images that were still playing across my thoughts. I run my hands up and down my body, trying to figure out if I was high, begging God to let it have only been a nightmare.

I race around my house and turn on every light. Staring at myself in the mirror, I search for signs that I've relapsed and weep with relief when I figure out that I haven't. The dreams were terrifying and stay with me long after I'm awake. Still, my ability to survive seems dependent on remembering the things I desperately want to forget. Yet, I lament the life I left behind and often wonder if the agony of the present is worth it.

Making peace with the loss of friendships has been difficult, even though relationships that began and ended with dope were never friendships at all. It's felt like the world is moving on without me, and I have no attachment to the people that live there. I've been stuck in this isolated bubble, floating around, trying to find a place that I fit.

I've spent a lot of time feeling sorry for myself instead of doing something to change my circumstances. Playing the victim is pretty natural to me after living in active addiction, and so is manipulating situations to get what I wanted. I quickly learn that getting clean doesn't suddenly give me a perfect life or solve all my problems. Even without meth, in many ways, I'm still a very sick woman.

Being alone and being lonely are not always the same thing. I'm not sure how to fill the void inside my soul, but there is a place I can go to meet people. There is an entire community of people just like me, drug addicts trying to stay clean, that would welcome me. So, I start attending twelve-step meetings regularly, and I start to make friends. The addicts I meet in these rooms would become some of the best people in my life—we just kind of click. There's respect, there's understanding, and there's love.

However, from the very beginning, my motives for attending

these meetings aren't strictly born from my desire to stay clean or even make friends; no, the driving factor is to meet men. I recognize that it isn't healthy or the behavior of somebody trying to change, but as I said, I'm still sick, just not dope sick.

I want to find a man to love me—somebody just like Cage, who looks like him, tattoos and all. Somebody who makes me feel the way he had. Bonus points if he spent time in prison. I don't know why that's a thing for me. One day, I'll want somebody that pays his taxes, has good credit, and no felonies.

In my head, the path of least resistance between being alone and being in love is sex. Internally, I wrestle with the part of my brain that knew better and the one that doesn't know any other way. I understood sex long before I even had the notion of what love was. I didn't date as many men as I wanted or screw as many as I could have, but I didn't do anything to heal the damaged parts of myself that I should have, either.

And then, I meet Andrew.

Andrew is also in recovery and the first man in my life that truly shows me that my value as a woman isn't dependent on how well I suck dick. He becomes a catalyst for changes that begin in my mind and, eventually, my spirit. And it all starts with him doing something no man had ever done.

He tells me no.

He won't sleep with me, but he will be my friend, and I'm honestly not sure what to make of any of it. Naturally, I'm confused, feel rejected, and assume that there was something very wrong with him. But he's hot, and I love having him around. And I know that eventually, I will wear him down, and he would be in my bed.

He often comes to my house, and we spend hours on my patio, talking about life and recovery. He sends me texts during the day to check on me, and I see him at meetings. He loves my dog, and Tempest loves him back. At night, we walk the trails and watch the fireflies fall out of the sky like stars and bounce around our feet.

His genuine interest and concern for my well-being are extraordinary for a woman like me. Like, he isn't pretending so that he can get into my pants; he really does care. He encourages me to get a sponsor and work the steps, and I decide to give it a go.

Her name is Betsy, and I'm intimidated by her gravitas. Also, her resting bitch face should be the one to which all others are compared. It takes some time before I ask her to sponsor me, sure that we couldn't possibly get along, but I was wrong. She's exactly what I need.

Having Andrew and Betsy in my life when I desperately need support, even if I haven't been willing to admit it, saves me from myself.

At least, for a little while.

13

RELAPSE

Charcoal clouds gather in the sky, and the wind howls, making the trees dance outside my window. I watch as the sky opens up and begins to weep, creating a hiss that steadily intensifies as the storm grows. Grimacing, I remember that I have once again screwed up by not listening to my mother; I still don't own an umbrella.

The room feels smaller than usual, and despite the storm roaring outside, it's stuffy and hot. Today, all the seats are full. People are lined up against the back wall and sitting on the floor. It's a good thing I arrived early because there is a one hundred percent chance that I wouldn't have stayed if I had to sit on the floor—especially during this meeting. It will last for an hour and a half; thirty minutes longer than most. Typically, I would avoid this one because Andrew never came, but Betsy had suggested that I come. And when I say she suggested, what I mean is that she directly said, "You better bring your ass to this meeting."

So, I brought my ass, and it is currently sitting in a hard plastic chair right next to my sponsor, falling asleep. I stare at the analog clock on the wall and follow the red hand as it completes a circle. And then another. The minute hand barely moves, mocking me, so I glare at it.

I'm startled out of my trance when whoever has been sharing starts to raise his voice. Choked with emotion, he sounds caught somewhere between bitter and devastated, his voice cracking on every word. I turn my head, shifting in my seat as I search for him. He is sitting a few chairs down from me on the room's left side, his head bowed. After a second, he raises his face, and I study it. I've never seen him before, but I feel instant empathy for his pain. My heart catches as I watch a single tear wind down the side of his cheek.

After wiping his face with the back of his hand, he looks back down and says, "I know that relapse is a part of recovery, but I am sick of messing up my life." He raises his head again. "Thanks for letting me share."

The place rustles as people shuffle in their seats, creating a ripple across the silent room.

Betsy quickly leans over and whispers to me. "No, relapse is *not* part of recovery; it's a *lack* of recovery."

I stare back at her and wonder why she had countered his statement. I let both of their words bounce around in my head. It takes a few minutes of mulling it over, but I'm reasonably sure I understand.

Saying that relapse is part of recovery implied that it happened to everybody and was expected of all addicts. Relapse is common, so his remark wasn't totally out of left field. Clearly, it was part of his story. However, I also understand why Betsy wanted to make the distinction clear. I haven't relapsed—at least not yet—and she didn't want me to plan on it just because so many fall off the wagon. I'm not sure what she meant by relapse being a lack of recovery, but I suspect that it had something to do with the book about the steps she gave me—the one I have yet to open. Regardless, she isn't going to give me permission or an excuse to go back out and start using again.

Looking around the room, I shiver as a morbid thought floats through my head; there are people in this room that will relapse, and some of them are going to die.

The next morning, I lie in bed, scrolling through Facebook with Tempest tucked up against me. My blinds are open, and beams of sunlight filter through, casting lines of shadow across the room. The storm passed in the middle of the night, and based on what the weather app has told me, today will be clear and beautiful.

I give my phone one last flick before getting up and starting my day. An image catches my eye before it disappears off the top of my screen, and I quickly scroll back to it. The image of a bright purple bicycle leaning against a concrete wall fills the small screen. It looks like a woman's bike, and the post says it's for sale—and cheap.

I have been thinking of buying a bike to ride with Mason on the trails behind our house, but they're expensive, and I'm poor as hell. Coming back from drug addiction is like starting in the negative; your credit is screwed, you have a massive gap in your work history, and you might have a history of evictions and endless unpaid bills racking up late fees. You might also have felonies, and nearly everyone has court fines they bounced out on.

Learning to live within a budget has been challenging, and it's not like I can sell dope or hustle for some extra cash. Well, I can, but I'm trying not to have any more charges on my record. So I've been taking random jobs to help supplement the money my mom gives me each month. I even lasted a few weeks digging ditches for a concrete company. It sucked, but I was able to buy Mason summer clothes, which made me pretty proud.

And my mom made me face the one thing that I was terrified of doing: check my credit. It was as bad as I knew it would be, and it's going to be a long battle in getting my shit together. But I do own a toaster now, so there's that.

I expand the post to see who's selling the bike, and my stomach drops. It's my friend, Marc. I met him a few months ago when I first started hitting meetings in the city. A huge giant of a man, he towers over everybody in the rooms. He's husky, bald, and reminds me of the bouncers for the clubs on Sunset Boulevard. He doesn't look like the kind of guy you would want to run into alone after dark, but once you get to know him, you realize he's one of the nicest guys in the world. Shy and quiet, he's incredibly sweet, and he has the best laugh, the contagious kind. He is just fun to be around.

We aren't best friends or lovers or anything, but we have spent time socializing in the same group of people, shared meals after meetings, and have become friends. He hasn't been out of prison for long, and I knew that attending meetings is a condition of his parole, but he seemed to be engaged and trying to stay out of trouble—until a few weeks ago when he stopped showing up. At first, I thought that maybe he found a job, and his schedule changed, but then one of the guys from his halfway house told me that he had been kicked out for popping dirty on a drug test.

And now he's selling his shit on social media—likely so that he can hustle up some cash for dope. We sold pieces of our life for pennies on the dollar to feed our habit, just par for the course when it came to addiction.

Without thinking it through, I shoot him a quick message, asking if the bike is still available. Purple isn't my favorite color, but I can tolerate it if it meant saving a hundred bucks. His reply comes seconds later, confirming that it was. I consider for a minute, then send my address and ask if he would deliver it. There's no way I can fit the bike into my tiny car. While I wait for his response, a nagging feeling begins to wedge itself into my thoughts. I'm pretty sure that this is the type of shit that I'm supposed to run by my sponsor before I do it.

It's easy to imagine how that conversation would go. Betsy would not be a fan of me inviting anybody that has possibly relapsed into my home. Not even for a discounted purple bike. She would be worried and advise me against this deal.

But I knew she doesn't have anything to worry about; I just want the bike, not dope.

Marc sends a response, letting me know he's on the way. It startles me to read that he is already coming; I'm still in bed, and it's pretty early in the morning. On the other hand, I remember how desperate I was when I needed money for dope. Jumping up, I scramble to get ready. I try to shake it, but a feeling of foreboding follows me as I walk down the stairs to meet Marc.

Twenty minutes later, I am standing in my open garage, watching Marc get out of a navy blue truck and walk towards me. I can tell that he is high.

"Hey, girl," he says, reaching for a hug.

Wrapping my arms around his neck, I give him a quick squeeze before pulling away. "How's it going, honey?"

"I'm makin' it. Just doing the best I can." Shaky, his words spill out rapidly, "Let me go grab the bike. Do you have the money?"

I nod and pull out the cash that I'd folded into my back pocket. As he reaches for it, I see his hand trembling, and his mouth is working in random jerking motions—the way that mine used to do too.

I suddenly realize I haven't been around anybody high since I got clean. At least, not outside of a meeting. People come into meetings all the time, clearly using, but they are likely there to get help and support. They are sick and tired of being sick and tired; they're desperate. Seeing them in that environment hits differently than when somebody is in your home, tweaking out right in front of you.

I watch him speed around in front of me, sputtering and moving erratically. He is speaking nonsense, and it's clear that he hasn't slept for a very long time. This should serve as a reminder of how far I've come and what I never want to be again, but it doesn't. Instead, it feels familiar, more so than the way I have been living since I stopped using drugs.

As he rolls my new bike toward me, I make an impulsive, stupid decision.

"Marc, do you think you could get me some shit?" The words are out of my mouth before I can stop them.

His mouth drops open. "Aren't you clean?"

"Yes, but..." Hesitating, I search for the right words. "Look, I've never had a relapse, and it's not like I want to start using again. I just want to do it one more time, to prove to myself that I can do it once and walk away." I'm not sure if I'm trying to convince him or myself.

He leans the bike just outside the entrance to my garage. "Babe, you don't want to do this."

"I have money."

Marc looks uncertain. "I don't have any on me. I would have to go get it."

"No problem. I'll give you the money, and you can just bring it to me—does that work?" I hold out my last fifty bucks. "Can you get me a few clean rigs too? I don't know how to get them here."

Slowly nodding, he takes the money. "It's going to be an hour or two. I'll call you when I'm on my way back." He turns around, gets into his truck, and drives away.

I stare after him and feel somewhere between excited and sick to my stomach. I walk to the bike and push it inside my garage and realize that the back tire is flat. Of course it is. Sighing loudly, I head back into my house and fall onto the couch.

I'm nervous and scared—I just set plans to relapse in motion. In my mind, I try to justify my behavior, feeling almost entitled to relapse. Everybody I know has relapsed at least once, but most went back out multiple times before they found long-term recovery. Why can't I? It almost doesn't seem fair. Besides, knowing what I know now about meth, I can do it just once and walk away. I'm not the same naïve chick I was years ago; I have experience. Dope isn't stronger than I am, right?

Over the next few hours, I don't leave my couch. I anxiously wait for Marc to call, checking my phone every five seconds. I decline the call from my mom and don't respond to either Andrew or Betsy's texts. I just want them all to leave me alone.

I see the notifications from Addict Chick and read the comments from strangers on the internet who found inspiration from the words I wrote. A sick feeling gnaws at my gut, and the more I read, the more ashamed I become. If I relapse, how could I possibly continue writing my book and posting about my recovery? I would be a total fake, and I wouldn't just disappoint my family; I would let down the thousands of people that follow me on social media. How can I even be considering getting high? After all these months of doing the right things, I decided to throw it all away in the space of a few minutes.

What the hell am I doing—have I learned nothing? Deep down, in the part of myself where honesty lives, I know the truth: I'm not stronger than dope, and one time will quickly turn into all the time. I will lose everything, including Mason. Nobody in the history of the world has ever been able to manage drug addiction. I would not be an exception.

Still, I keep checking my phone. In one breath, I pray to God that Marc won't call. In the next, I hope he will. If he does, I'm going to be getting high tonight. Even with months of clean time under my belt, I'm still powerless when it comes to dope. My relapse will be decided by fate.

My phone rings—it's Marc. I feel my heart race, my adrenaline spreading through me, and I'm terrified. Chewing on my lower lip, I feel like my soul is being torn apart. Answering is deciding to throw my life away, but I'm not strong enough to decline it.

Against my own volition, my finger clicks the button to accept the call. "Hey."

"Girl, you are going to hate me and think I'm the biggest piece of shit… but I'm not getting you anything." He speaks at a million miles per hour, barely breathing between words. "You're doing so good. You don't want this life." He pauses, taking a breath. "I'm not even sorry, but I'm not giving the money back."

"Keep it." The loss of fifty dollars was small compared to what I could have lost. "And Marc? Thank you."

As I hang up, relief hits me in sharp waves. I lean back onto the couch and cry. I feel like a total failure; I'm so ashamed. The balance of my life had hinged on a drug addict who has denied me dope. I have little doubt that keeping the money was a huge motivation not to supply me with meth, but I would like to believe that in some part of his addicted mind, he really feels like he did it because I couldn't do it for myself.

I'll never know for sure. A few days later, Marc died of an overdose.

14
AUTHORSHIP

Excerpt from *Addict Chick: Sex, Drugs & Rock 'N Roll*

She is leaning against her black Volkswagen EOS at the gas station, filling it up. It's early morning, and the sun is just beginning to come up over the horizon. The grass is wet with dew, and the rays from the sun are shining through the water, creating sparkling prisms of light. It's beautiful, and she doesn't know how she could have ever possibly doubted the existence of God. The city of Lexington, Kentucky, is just starting to wake up, the roads slowly filling with cars headed to church.

She began to muse over the last four years of her life. She thinks back and remembers the first moments of falling in love, the heady feeling of knowing she had found her soul mate. She smiles at the memories that flood her mind. She had been so happy. But then her heart drops, remembering how that love had turned into hate and how her life had become a living nightmare. An existence filled with pain, anger, and sickness, shadowed by unbearable loss and shame.

Then she remembers that without the nightmare, she never would have found her way to God. She knows now that she would never have become who she was meant to be without living through hell. She could never appreciate everything life had to offer if she hadn't lost everything she had. She could not have known the value of life until she had died. And she could not have loved herself until she had lost herself. And here she was, happy and whole and in love with a life that she so easily could have never had. She knew she was blessed, far more than she deserved.

It's cool, and the wind is blowing her black hair into her face. It's a wild mess, flying unchecked. She doesn't try and push it back; instead, she lets it tickle her nose. She smiles and thinks about the wind and how it surrounds her now. She wonders if Cage can feel it too. She wonders if he remembers the life they had before drugs destroyed it.

She gets in her car and starts it. The engine hums quietly, and she feels the power beneath her ass. Her heart is full, and her mind resolute. She is finally ready. She turns out of the gas station and jumps onto the freeway, headed west. She was headed to Texas.

Headed to Cage.

As I travel the miles toward Cage, I think about my life now. I've been clean for over seven months, and in that time, I wrote an entire book, got my kid back, and started to build a beautiful new life. Kentucky is much different than Texas, but I'm happy there. It feels safe and exactly where I should be. I know that I can find dope anywhere I go, but as the days and months have gone by, I think of it less and less.

I've made some fantastic friends and have good people in my life—people that care and love me. It's been an extraordinary thing to build relationships that aren't predicated on using drugs together. Now, my circle is full of people on the same mission as me—to stay clean.

Something that I never expected, but has had such a significant impact on my recovery, is the people I've met across social media—especially through my Addict Chick page. Every day, I get to interact and engage with people worldwide that share my struggles and offer me support in ways that I'll never be able to explain.

I'm so proud of the life I've created, and I cannot wait to see Cage tomorrow and share it with him. It will be the first time he has seen me clean in nearly five years. I've been waiting for this moment since the second I put down the dope. I've finally done everything that I had spent years promising him I would do. Tomorrow will be the beginning of our new life together. I have no idea how we will manage living apart once he gets out of prison, but we'll figure it out.

Glancing out the window of my car, I see the sun come out from behind white clouds, the pattern of the beams making designs on my dashboard. I absorb the warmth as I watch the miles go by, lost in thought.

Just as I am crossing over the Mississippi River on the

Hernando de Soto Bridge—the bridge that connects West Memphis, Arkansas, and Memphis, Tennessee—my phone rings. I reach for it and check the display. Excited, I quickly accept the call.

"Cage," I say, a smile already plastered across my face.

"Hey, baby, can you talk?" His voice sounds strange, and I start to get a sick feeling inside my gut.

"Yep, I'm in the car on my way to see you." Silence fills the line, making me feel sicker still. "I'll be there tomorrow, and I can't wait to suck your face off," I add, pretending that everything is okay, even though I can tell it isn't.

"Wind, I got your letter. I'm sorry, but you're not going to be able to get in to see me." He doesn't sound sorry at all.

"Wait, what are you talking about? Why not?"

"Because you're not on my visitor's list. I didn't add you when I transferred to this unit, and I'm only allowed to make changes once every six months."

I shake my head, trying to sort the implications of what he is telling me before I go crazy, but my anger bubbles to the surface. "Wow, Cage. I'm halfway there!" It isn't exactly accurate, but close enough. "Why didn't you call me or write to me?"

"I'm calling you now," he says, and his voice takes on a hard edge.

"Yeah, after I rearranged my schedule and started driving across the country to see you," I grumble. "There's no way you can fix this so I can come tomorrow?"

"No," he says. He doesn't give a damn that he's just crushed me. "And there probably won't be time to get you on the list before I get out."

"So, I won't get to see you at all?"

"You can come to see me when I get out. That would be better for me, anyway."

The sudden coolness in his voice confuses me. The last time we talked, he was excited about me coming to see him. Our last few letters to each other were all good. I don't know what has changed, but clearly, something has.

"What's wrong with you? Talk to me, Cage. I can tell something is going on."

"I just don't want to see you. Not now." His words remind me of his trademark cruelty. "Look, I'm glad you're still clean and have this awesome new life while I'm still stuck in prison."

Now I understand, and the guilt comes at me in waves. While I have gotten clean and started over, Cage is still dealing with the consequences of the choices we made—choices that I set in motion. He's bitter and resentful, and I can't blame him.

"I understand," I say as I choke back tears, "and again, I'm so sorry—about everything. I hate that you're there, and I wish I could go back and change what happened. But I can't. I hope that when you get out, I can see you, and we can fix all of this. I love you so much. I really do."

His voice softens, and I can feel his remorse through the phone. "Wind, I love you too. I don't know how I'm going to feel when I get out. So much has happened between us. There's so much I don't know—shit I might never know. I don't know if we can go back. I don't know if I even want to."

The tears come now, silently falling down my face. I pull my car onto the shoulder of the highway and turn on my hazards before I can cause a twenty car pile-up. "You're breaking my heart right now. We're both finally clean. Please don't give up on us."

"I'm not—I just need some time, Wind."

"Okay, I'll do my best to give that to you." In my heart, I don't know how I could survive if he decides that he doesn't want me anymore. "The book is finally done. I'm going to mail you one of the first copies. Maybe, once you read it, it will answer some of the questions you have."

"I'm not sure if I want to read it, but I'll try. Even if I don't, I want you to know that I'm proud of you. I know you're wicked smart, but writing a book couldn't have been easy. You're doing good, don't mess it up." He sounds like he means it.

"I won't—promise," I say, smiling through my tears.

"Look, I'm sorry you made the trip for nothing. You need to turn around and go back to Kentucky; Texas isn't good for you. I'll write to you soon. I love you, Wind."

"I love you, too," I say, but he's already hung up.

Sitting on the side of the road somewhere in Arkansas, I fall apart. I feel my heart crack in two, and I just weep. I can't believe that this is happening. I need him to see me clean; it's more than just important; it's everything. If he could look at my face and hear the truth in my voice, it would fix everything. We're both finally back to the people we were before the drugs, so can't we just go back to the way we used to be?

It seems so simple, but if I'm honest with myself, I know it's not. We might be clean now, but we aren't the same people anymore. At least, I know that I'm not. Even so, my love for Cage hasn't changed. If anything, I'm even more in love with him now. And I know that he loves me. So, why do I suddenly have the feeling that this is goodbye? Like—for good.

I take a deep breath and push that ugly thought out of my head before it makes me throw myself in front of a passing semi. I take a look at my surroundings; I don't want to die in Arkansas. But do I keep going to Texas or do what Cage told me to do and turn around? I'm equidistant between my mom's house and my place in Kentucky.

I mull it over, laying out the pros and cons in my mind. I haven't seen my mom in forever, and she is expecting me, but Texas isn't as appealing if I can't see Cage. On the other hand, I miss my dog and my house, but Mason is already with his dad, and I would be alone in Kentucky.

Next, I weigh what has typically been the deciding factor in many of the choices I've made—men. In Kentucky, Andrew still hasn't come around, and there isn't anybody else there I want to have sex with. I've realized that using meetings to find men for sex is a terrible idea for my recovery. Most of the men I know are recently clean, like me, and there aren't enough degrees of separation between dope sex and regular sex. The few times I've been to bed with somebody, I had this sick fantasy that the sex wasn't as good as it would've been if we were high. So, I've decided to at least try not to have sex with men that have only been clean for a few months. I probably shouldn't even date anybody that has ever done drugs—that would be safer for somebody like me—but I'm still on the fence about it. I don't know anybody that isn't a recovering drug addict, and I'm not ready to become a nun and give up sex altogether.

I review my options in Texas and have the same problem. In the past, I had plenty of lovers that weren't addicts, but there isn't anybody for whom I felt like driving six hours to and twelve hours back, either.

This is a bizarre situation for me to be in; I can't remember a time when I didn't have lovers stacked up and ready to go. I mean, I do not doubt that I could find one if I want one, but I honestly don't want one. The revelation shocks and confuses me. There is something wrong with me, and I have no idea what to do with any of this. It's a little too much for me to examine in the middle of Bill Clinton's birthplace, so I shake it off and start my engine.

I drive off the shoulder and head the way I had been going—to Texas. Cage told me to turn around, but I'm not down for anybody to tell me what to do anymore—especially a man.

I'm going to do whatever I want, and I want to go home.

15

TRADING THE SPOON FOR THE FORK
PRESENT DAY

I'm about to get vulnerable, a little shallow, and very honest.

I've been clean for over five years at the time of writing this book, and it's been a long time since I have wanted to get high. I no longer crave the feeling of being blasted out of my mind; I remember the racing of my heart and debilitating anxiety and paranoia. I don't wish for the artificial energy that meth gave me; I remember the terrible things I used to do when I was awake. I have zero desire to ever experience meth sex again in my life; I remember the vile and revolting woman I became. The further away I've gotten from the last time, the more evident it's become that there is absolutely nothing that I miss about meth.

Well, except for that one thing. Even after all this time, I still yearn for the body that dope gave me. Hell, I dream about it. There have been more times than I would like to admit that I have seriously considered going back on the meth diet. I have examined that scenario in my head from every direction, and I can promise that if there were a way to do it just for weight loss and without burning my entire life to the ground, it would be a done deal.

Sometimes I see pictures of myself from back then and make comments like, "God, I looked terrible when I was using drugs," or "I did not look good that skinny." You know what? I'm totally lying. Every. Single. Time. There isn't one picture from my dope days that features a body I wouldn't rather still have.

When I say body, I do mean from the neck down. I prefer my face now over the one I had in those days because nothing can age you quicker than methamphetamine. I sported permanent dark circles under my eyes, giving me a haunted look. I was gaunt and with no fat to fill my face out, wrinkles formed and aged me by years, nearly overnight. But the rest of my body? It was bangin'.

Half a decade after getting clean, and this is still a legitimate struggle in my life. Crazy, right? I'm not saying this affects everybody that gets clean or sober because—well, because I'm not everybody. But for me and many women I know, weight gain is the most challenging part of recovery. And there are a substantial number of people that relapse and die over it.

For as long as I can remember, I was overweight. I'm pretty sure I was even a fat baby. Growing up, I wasn't athletic or active, always preferring to have my nose stuck in a book over anything else. In my family, we celebrated everything with food. I discuss this more in-depth later in the book, but I used food as a coping strategy to escape the pain of ongoing sexual trauma in my childhood. Of course, I didn't know that until after hours of therapy as an adult.

My brothers teased me, the way brothers do, but I never knew I was fat until a girl told me so when I tried to join the swim team in elementary school. Once during a classroom Halloween party, a teacher took away my candy bag and told me that I didn't need candy; I needed a diet.

I won't say that I didn't have friends in middle school because I did—I was even in the popular crowd. My friends were beautiful, but I never resented them for any of it. Well, I was jealous of Kim Poole's long legs and Monica Beltran's exotically beautiful face. I was lucky to discover a group of girls that I built lifelong friendships with, but I was always the fat friend back then.

In high school, I never had a boyfriend. I couldn't even find a date for my senior prom, so my cousin Meghan asked her boyfriend to take me since they went to a different school and had their dance on a different night. Out of pity, or maybe because he was just a good guy, he took me.

I have always had confidence in other areas of my life, but I never once felt comfortable with my body or how I looked—until I started using meth. I'm sure my newfound confidence came partly from the dope, but there is no denying that going from a size fourteen to a size three also played a part. I'm not going to go into all the ways I used that body when I was on dope—if you have ever done meth, you already know.

One of the most significant objections I had for getting clean was gaining weight—it's pretty much guaranteed to happen. Again, most people that have used drugs can relate to this. When I entered treatment, I tried very hard to stay in front of the inevitable; I worked out every day and tried to stay away from sugar. I was pretty successful, but once I was out of that controlled environment, it was game over.

I was off the dope and onto the cheesecake. For the first few months, I didn't care. Drug addiction and eating processed foods have similar effects on the brain—they both trigger the release of dopamine. I couldn't have dope, I shouldn't have dick, so food became the next best thing. I read a study once that said Oreos light up the brain reward system just as much as cocaine. I'm pretty sure that Baskin-Robbins does the same thing. I was learning how to live my life without drugs, but I was not learning how to take care of myself.

It is normal to gain weight when you get clean and sober, but that doesn't make it any easier to deal with. And it's not like the weight all came back overnight, but one day I woke up and not even my panties fit me anymore. That was the day that I started to see myself the way I used to be before drugs. And I began to contemplate relapsing—just so that I could lose the weight.

My self-worth is so wrapped up in the size of my body that there have been times I would willingly throw away my clean time just to be a few sizes smaller. I absolutely know how terrible that sounds, but I hope that somebody reading this can relate and see that I've still managed to make it this far without relapsing, despite the way I sometimes feel.

Yes, I've read the books on self-love and seen the memes on Facebook about the importance of accepting yourself for who you are and how learning to love yourself is the best thing you can do. It sounds so easy, but it turns out applying it in your life is far more complicated. I realize that feelings aren't facts, and the way I see myself isn't necessarily the way other people see me. I know I'm stuck with the person I am, but I am not stuck with the body I have—at least, not *all* the body I have. Those are the things that I try to focus on.

I've learned to accept that being fat is hard, getting fit is hard, and ultimately, I have to pick my hard. I hate working out, and I think that people who say they love it are lying their asses off. Except maybe my friend Dr. Cali Estes, but she's a freak. Anyway, I hate working out, and I kind of suck at it, but I do it because it makes a difference in the way I feel.

I'm fully aware that my self-esteem, or lack of it, is a very dangerous part of who I am. It's caused unrepairable damage in many of my relationships. Many of the poor choices I've made stem directly from my inability to see my value beyond the way I look.

Being aware of my issues has allowed me to work on them. I keep a journal of self-affirmations, and I try to write in it every day. I know that I'm smart, kind, and a good mom. I'm healthy, my family is healthy, I have a great job, and people that care about me.

See what I did there? I pulled that shit right out of the journal.

I wish I had been able to write this chapter with all of the answers, but as you can tell, I'm still trying to figure it out for myself. I just want you to know that you aren't alone. Nothing about staying clean is easy. We will struggle, and some days we're going to want to give up and give in. But if I've learned anything at all over the last five years, it's that hanging on through those moments, even when you feel like you have no reason to keep going, is what matters. Nothing is ever as bad as you think it is, and there are very few things you can't come back from or fix—unless you're dead.

I now try very hard not to obsess with the size of my body. Instead, I try to focus on the health of my body; I want to be around for Mason and my future grandchildren for a very long time. I'm never going to have the body I had when I was on drugs because I'm never going to be on drugs again. Being a few pounds overweight isn't the worst-case scenario, but relapsing and losing everything I've worked so hard for would be.

16

YEAR ONE

Andrew sits next to me on the couch, downing his second cup of coffee and watching me over the rim of his mug. Tempest is sprawled out beside him with her head on his lap, and he absentmindedly strokes her neck. There aren't many people in the world who my dog would choose to sit next to over me; Andrew is most definitely one of them. Disloyal bitch.

We had gotten back to my house a little while ago, and I was still smiling so hard that my cheeks ached. What a magical freaking day. I could live another hundred years, and there will never be another day that feels quite like this one; there couldn't be. You only make it to a year clean for the first time once. Even if the worst happens and I relapse one day, coming back and making it to a year again wouldn't feel like this.

When I first got clean, the goal was just to make it twenty-four hours, but there were more than a few times that the best I could do was make it ten more minutes. Those minutes often felt like days. The physical symptoms of suddenly denying my body meth were rough. Not as bad as they would've been if I were withdrawing from opiates or alcohol, but still pretty awful. I was so exhausted that I would sleep for hours, but it wasn't an escape because nightmares plagued me every moment my eyes were closed. I would wake up screaming, completely drained of energy. I would lay in puddles of sweat, unable to move at all. I had a headache for weeks, and no matter how much I ate, I was never satisfied. I moved through the days like a zombie, stumbling through a foggy field, and everything seemed surreal.

But the pain and discomfort of my body was nothing compared to the visceral torture inside my mind. It was hell. I don't know how else to describe it; it was a living, breathing nightmare. The only thought I could muster up was that I needed dope. If I could just do a shot, I would be able to get out of bed, go to the bathroom, get dressed, and get myself together. I was convinced that if I could get high, just once more, then I would be able to get clean. That was the message circulating inside my brain for days, and I begged God just to let me die so the misery could end.

Somehow, I crawled my way into thirty days, but I vacillated between holding on and giving up so many times that nobody was more shocked than me when I received my green key tag at sixty days clean. Two months. Then three, four, five, and six months, and all the hours between contained emotions that I hadn't felt in years. They were terrifying, but none more so than the feelings that evoked a positive reaction. I understood pain, guilt, and shame—I had been living those for my entire addiction. But joy, happiness, and contentment? Those were foreign, and I didn't feel like I deserved to have anything good in my life. The overwhelming urge to self-sabotage during that time very nearly took me out.

There were days and weeks of frustration leading into months seven, eight, and nine because once the euphoric cloud of being clean had passed, the days dragged by, monotonous, and often boring. Real-life felt stagnant and just kind of sucked. I had finished writing *Addict Chick: Sex, Drugs & Rock 'N Roll*, so my motivation to get up in the morning was just gone. I felt like I was losing myself and had no idea what direction to take. When I talked to my mom about it, she reminded me that I needed to focus on the day in front of me instead of worrying about tomorrow. She used the analogy that John Steinbeck only wrote one page a day—and some of his novels are hundreds of pages long—so every day, I should focus on writing a page instead of an entire book.

The most challenging part of this year was that I expected to become a whole different person almost overnight without doing the work to get there. The days passed, and while I was clean, I didn't feel like anything else was changing. But in the last few days, I've looked back and taken a mental inventory of this year and have realized that there haven't been just little changes; rather, *everything* has changed. It was hard to see when I was taking it only one day at a time, but the culmination of those days added up to an entirely new life—a beautiful, badass life.

I've made it a year without meth, holding on when I wanted to give up. I haven't relapsed, even when I wanted to. I'm a mother again and a loving daughter. I launched a social media brand and met awe-inspiring people. I wrote a book and started my life over with less than nothing. It had been a beautiful, glorious, and extraordinary year—capped off with a celebration, meeting, and food, surrounded by a group of addicts that had grown to be my family.

I have been to many clean-time birthday celebrations over the last year, and I'm not sure if 'envy' would be the right word, but I wanted to experience whatever those people must have felt. You could see it on their faces; gratitude, yes—and pride—but it was so much more than that. Now, I know what that was: wonder. The real feelings laid hidden within the wonder of all they had accomplished.

There had been decorations and balloons tied to my chair, and Mason had sat proudly beside me. Betsy and Andrew stood up and said the most beautiful and kind things, completely humbling me. And there were freaking presents! Betsy gave me this beautiful bracelet with black and translucent white beads and skull charms. It was gorgeous and utterly me. There were a million hugs and so much love; I spent most of the night on the verge of tears. All the way home, I replayed the night in my head.

Now, setting his coffee on the table, Andrew reaches into his pocket and hands something to me. It's a black, velvet bag that looks like a little envelope with the logo of our fellowship imprinted in gold on the front.

"What's this?" I ask.

"It's for you, silly. Open it up."

Tucking my thumb under the flap, I flip it open and turn it over. Something drops into my outstretched hand. Raising it to my face, I look at the gold and black coin, blinged-out with silver glitter, and tears well up in my eyes. I got my glow-in-the-dark one-year key tag during my birthday celebration, but this medallion is something else altogether. On one side was written "God-Service-Society-Self," surrounding the number one. Flipping the coin over, I read the words, and they are immediately ingrained in my mind: "That No Addict Seeking Recovery Need Ever Die…"

I look up at him. "Andrew, I don't know what to say." And the tears that had been welling since I opened the package finally escape from my lower lid and stream down my face.

Andrew shrugs, but a slow smile works its way across his face and into his eyes. "I'm proud of you." He pulls me into his arms and hugs me tightly against his body. It's the perfect end to a perfect day.

Or, it would have been a perfect day.

Seconds after telling Andrew goodbye and shutting the front door, my phone rings. Spinning around so fast I nearly fall over, I rush across the room to pick it up, already smiling before seeing the number on the screen.

Cage.

I knew he would call; I've been expecting it all day. He knows what today means and how important it is to me—to us both.

I cross to the couch as I go through the automated prompts and impatiently wait to be connected.

"Wind." As usual, his voice makes my breath catch.

"Hey! I've been waiting all freaking day for you to call!"

"I know. We weren't allowed to get on the phones until just a little bit ago," he explains. "But congratulations! You made it. How does it feel?"

"Honestly, the day has been overwhelming, but also really amazing. Mason went with me to the celebration, and it's been magical."

"I'm happy for you—I really am. Staying clean is tough, but you did it."

The tone of his voice sounds off, strained, somehow. I ignore it, refusing to acknowledge that anything might be wrong—not today, of all days.

"So, did you get my book? I sent it a few weeks ago, but you never responded to my letters, so I thought maybe the jail wouldn't let you have it or something." I have been waiting for him to call and say something about the book. I've been nervous for him to read it, but one of the biggest reasons I started writing it was so that he would know everything. Especially how much I love him.

After a brief hesitation, Cage finally speaks. "Yes, I got it." His voice is changing into something I recognize—anger.

I open my mouth to speak and then stop, waiting for him to continue. The place in my chest—the one that sits below my heart and above my belly button—begins to fill with fire and acid. I feel sick.

"That's really why I wanted to call you tonight. I can't believe you wrote that shit and thought I would want to read it." He isn't screaming. Instead, his tone is chilling, and I feel a shiver run up my back and into my throat. "You're a bitch for sending that to me. What the hell is wrong with you? Did you really think that I would want to read about you being a whore?"

The world tilts. I don't know how to respond. I was an idiot for thinking that Cage wanted to know everything; of course, he didn't. I misjudged the entire situation, and now it's irreparable. I can't take back the words I wrote because I had the bright idea to publish them all in a book. A book that Cage has now read. There's no undoing that.

"Cage, I'm— "

"Fuck you."

"—sorry."

"No, don't say you're sorry. You've said enough."

I take a deep breath and release it slowly, trying to get myself under control before I start to cry. "Listen, please," I plead, sounding as desperate as I felt, "I am sorry. I thought you wanted to know everything. I knew the sex would bother you, but is that all you got out of the entire book? Did you not read about how much I love you?"

"Wind, I didn't need to read about that in a book. I've always known that. Jesus, you wrote the book to hurt me."

"That isn't true, I swear. I thought if I was honest and told you everything, then you would stop agonizing over shit that had never happened."

"You should have left me to my imagination because what I thought happened wasn't as disgusting as what actually happened. You were mine, and now all I can think about is another man touching you. You spared no details on that shit. I will never forgive you—not ever."

I can't hold back the tears anymore, and they cascade down my face as I fold into myself.

"You've changed. And I'm not talking about when you were on dope—I'm talking about now," he says, sounding less pissed off and more bitter. "You've been clean for a year now, and every time you send me a letter or I call you, you feel different. You're not the same woman I fell in love with."

"That isn't fair, Cage." My voice sounds like it was coming from my nose over the tears, "I am the same woman, at least in how much I still love you. This entire year I've laid in bed, imagining you getting out and us starting our lives together. I've finally done everything you always wanted me to do."

"I never wanted you to write a book."

"So you're throwing 'us' away over a book?"

He hesitates. "No, I'm throwing 'us' away over what you wrote in that book. And I don't just mean all the sex you had with other men. I realized something else when I read it. I don't think we could stay clean together. I mean, when you were writing it, didn't you see that we had spent more time together on drugs than we did without?" After another pause, he takes a breath. "I'm sorry, Wind, we're over. There is never going to be an 'us' ever again." I can hear the ache in his voice, but I also hear the finality—he means it

It's over. My heart breaks at the thought, but it terrifies me too. Who am I without Cage? I want to beg him not to do this, but the words don't make it past my lips because he's right. Cage dared to say what I have refused to acknowledge—even though it has been living on the side of my consciousness for months. Too much time has passed, and there has been far too much damage done. We are toxic to each other, and no amount of clean time could change that. Even though I don't want to, I understand what he is doing—the right thing for both of us.

"I love you, Cage. I'm so sorry."

"I'm sorry too." I can hear the tears in his voice now—and the heartbreak. "I'm getting out in a few days, and I can't do this with you anymore. I want to stay clean and get my life together. I can't do that with you. Please, stay away and let me just move on with my life."

Silence.

Our connection is broken, and I stare down at my phone, shocked. There are so many things I still want—no need—to say, but it feels like my brain has frozen.

And then I remember that I can email him, and he would receive it before he is released. Even though he asked me to leave him alone, I need to do this. Cage knows me well enough that he'll expect it.

```
Dear Cage,
    After your call, I needed to send you
this last letter. After this, I promise
you will never hear from me again because
I realized that you're right-relapsing
```

together would be worse than living without you. I'm devastated, and I feel like I'm dying, but I also know that this is the right thing to do. We loved deep and hard, and there just isn't any going back for us.

I know I've changed, but so have you. I may not be the same girl you met all those years ago, but I wouldn't have become the person I am without you. Meeting and falling in love with you changed the course of my life—even fifty years from now, you will still be part of who I am.

I wish we could go back—even if it ended the way it's ending today—I could relive that first year with you over and over again.

The most painful part of this is that I never got to see you after I got clean, and it's ripping me apart that the last memory you have of me is sitting across from you in jail while I was high and strung-out. That is going to haunt me until the day I die.

I hope that when you think of me, you think of the woman I was before drugs—the woman that truly loved you. Please don't forget her. There are so many things I want to say, but I think you already know. We will always have a connection, and neither of us will ever be able to feel the wind and not think about the other. I find comfort in that.

Always know that I'm rooting for you, praying for you, and I want you to make it. I want you to get out in a few days and start a beautiful, badass life, and I mean that with all my heart.

I won't ever forget you or the way we loved each other.

Goodbye, Cage.

Love,
   Wind.

I send the final letter and just sit there, staring into space. I feel lost—like I'm traveling into nothing. My emotional commitment to Cage has been cut, and nothing is tethering me to the world anymore. If somebody had told me a year ago that this would be the way my first year would end, I wouldn't have believed them.

There has never been a time—not during the years of active addiction, until right this second—that I ever considered that Cage and I wouldn't find our way back to each other. Never in a million years did I think that our love would come down to a moment like this. I want to grab the hands of time and rewind them past the point in our relationship when it had become too late. Letting my brain retreat to our memories together, I go back to the beginning, trying to find the moment fate had decided that we were too far gone.

The truth collides into my denial, obliterating the barrier of lies I had built around myself.

I have been holding onto a fantasy, a dream, because Cage and

I never had a chance once we started getting high together. Our future together died that day, burned down to smoldering embers, and I have been standing beside the cinders ever since, trying to stay warm. Everything I want isn't just gone, it's gone forever, and it was destroyed years ago. I feel like I'm just waking up, and somebody else has been living my life and doing a terrible job. I shake my head to try and clear the thoughts that are about to drown me.

Casting my eyes down, I see the book sitting in the middle of the coffee table before me. The cover is blood red, and the title reads *Addict Chick: Sex, Drugs & Rock 'N Roll* in a scrolling white font. I pull it into my lap and stare at it. The silence of the room presses into me, and I can hear my heartbeat inside my head.

Oh. My. God. I made a monumental mistake when I wrote the epilogue in the book. I had eluded to the happy freaking ending that everybody always expects when they read a story because I had been confident that there would be one. And I had been wrong—my destiny isn't with Cage. The arc of our love story would die within these pages. Nausea rolls through me, and the cake from earlier threatens to make an appearance.

Tonight, after the meeting, a chick asked me how I had managed to make it an entire year without getting high. I told her that I went to meetings regularly, got a sponsor, and worked the steps—which was true, although I hadn't made it through the steps yet. Still, attending meetings and surrounding myself with other addicts had been a big part of how I had gotten to this night without relapsing, but it wasn't the only reason.

I'm a mom again, and building a life with my son is the most significant gift of my recovery. Learning to be a parent has been challenging—Mason drives me crazy every single day, but I wouldn't trade those moments for anything. With a lot of hard work and time, I've finally earned back Daniel's trust too.

I'm a daughter again. I'm no longer the reason that my mom cries. We're making brand new memories together, and her love, support, and faith have provided a foundation that has enabled me to start over.

The connections I've built with the people across my social media have gotten me through some challenging moments. The longer I've stayed clean and the more content I've created and pushed out, the more compelled I've felt to remain clean. Yes, there have been moments over the last year that I've felt resentful; the pressure of so many people counting on me to stay clean was overwhelming but also empowering. I wanted other women to look at me and see that you can come back from addiction, work hard, regain everything you've lost, and build an even more badass life.

Lost in thoughts about worldly things, guilt begins to inch into my chest. I need to get honest with myself. The biggest reason I am sitting here, still clean, is God. Twelve months after begging him to save my life, I'm still alive, and I haven't relapsed. Hadn't I even written a book about how my addiction had led me right to the feet of Jesus? A book that, even while I wrote it, I knew wouldn't be pleasing to God? I mean, I'm pretty sure he would've objected to the chapter I had devoted to squirting.

And I've done nothing in all of this time to build a relationship with God. I've been to church a handful of times but still haven't opened a Bible. At night, when I remember to pray, it's usually to ask for help with something, and I sound like an idiot. Over the last year, I have had multiple instances where I nearly relapsed, and I told myself that I had just gotten lucky. But was it luck, or was it God saving me from myself?

Trying to reconcile my failure as a delivered Christian woman on the same night that my dreams of the future were shattered is too much. I would not be finding atonement, and thinking about all the ways I have let God down, makes the shame in my soul begin to grow.

I've often heard that the first year of recovery is the most difficult to get through, but if you manage to drag yourself through those twelve months, recovery would get easier. Would it, though? So much of the last year has been predicated on knowing that staying clean was the only way to get my old life back, the life I had before I became a meth addict. Getting back to Cage propelled me through this year, and now that motivation is gone. How would I stay clean now?

Tempest rests her head on my leg, and I stroke the side of her face, bringing myself back to the present. I take a deep breath and focus on who I am now, not who I used to be. Cage was right; I have changed. In many ways, I'm a completely different person than the woman who had fallen for him. The identity that had been irrevocably tied to our relationship is suddenly independent, and I'm evolving and growing more every single day.

No, I don't think recovery is ever going to be easy, no matter how long I stay clean. But, I have learned an even more important lesson—I will get stronger.

17

CHILDHOOD TRAUMA
PRESENT DAY

If you've read my first book, you know that I was raped by a group of neighborhood boys when I was six years old and that the abuse continued for years. My first experience in forming relationships began with those boys. I was granted friendship and attention in exchange for the use of my body. Before I wrote about it in *Sex, Drugs & Rock 'N Roll*, there had been very few people in my life that even knew about the things that happened back then because I barely even remembered it myself. I knew that the assaults had happened, but the memories were separated inside my mind as though they belonged to somebody else.

Childhood should be a time of innocence; kids are supposed to feel safe and protected. Children process information differently from adults, so when our sense of safety is shattered by trauma, we adapt to the circumstances. For me, experiencing ongoing sexual trauma when I was so young, during the time I was forming my core beliefs about how the world worked, shaped the woman I grew up to be. My identity development was viciously interrupted and changed the way I learned to see myself.

Our brains are extraordinary, and after the first rape, my mind worked to protect itself by disassociating from the experience and repressing the memory. My coping mechanism was to take the experience, drop it into a box inside my head, paint it yellow, and toss it out of my thoughts. Over the years, there have been times that the recollections would come back in pieces, like emotional flashbacks. I would see them littered on the floor of my mind, often out of order. Fragments of memory that could elicit a feeling of shame so powerful that I would quickly sweep them up, put them back in the box, and toss them out again.

I kept those memories buried as deeply as possible, and they would probably still be there if my therapist in rehab hadn't dragged them out. The recommendation was that I continued intense trauma therapy when I got out of treatment, but I didn't listen. Instead, I decided that acknowledging that the abuse happened was enough. I felt like it had happened so long ago that no amount of therapy was going to change anything.

I then wrote *Addict Chick Sex, Drugs & Rock 'N Roll* and recounted the details of my sexual trauma. I don't regret writing about the abuse because I've had many women reach out to me with stories similar to my own. However, I wish I had written it after I had gotten help. When I read the book now, I can see that it was written by a woman whose childhood trauma had turned into adult manifestations. For as long as I can remember, my natural response to pretty much everything in my life has been to sexualize it—the more obscene and shocking, the better. Sex was the answer to love, happiness, anger, fear, danger, and self-worth. I feel like I even sexualized the rapes when I wrote about them. Not intentionally, but it's evident to me now that I was still very sick.

I have always wondered who I would be and how I would have turned out if I hadn't had those experiences as a child. How would my life be different today if none of that had happened? Would I have ever used drugs or fallen in love with Cage? What if I had gotten help when I was younger, while there was still time to change the person I became? I've driven myself crazy with thoughts like that, usually when I find myself in a situation that I know is a result of my unresolved childhood trauma.

I didn't seek help when I left treatment. If I had, then I think I would be writing a very different book today. I didn't truly begin to advocate for my mental health until about a year ago—four years after I got clean and thirty-five years after the trauma started. It took the destruction of my marriage and losing a man I truly loved to finally accept that I needed help. I would never have a chance at a healthy relationship if I didn't address the nightmares that still lived in the darkest corners of my mind.

The life I lived between when I wrote SDRR and *unCaged* is a story that deserves a book all its own. One day, I'll write it because it's a very important part of my life. During that time, I met and married a man named Ivey. I've never met anybody like him, and there has never been or will ever be a man who loved me the way he did. It's hard for me to even write his name right here because thinking about all the ways I sabotaged my one chance at happiness is enough to make me cry. But losing Ivey was the catalyst for me finally getting help.

About a year ago, I started seeing a therapist because I knew that my life would never change if I didn't deal with my past. My official diagnosis was Childhood Sexual Abuse (CSA) related Complex Post-Traumatic Stress Disorder (C-PTSD). During treatment, I came to terms with the fact that so much of my life and the choices I make, stems from my childhood. The way I learned to give and receive love was through sex, and that is obviously not the way it's supposed to work.

I loved having somebody that was forced to listen to me talk for fifty minutes, because I paid them to, but the progress was pretty slow and I didn't feel any different. I decided to go back to the therapy that I had begun when I was in rehab—Eye Movement Desensitization and Reprocessing (EMDR) therapy, and it changed my life. I don't know how to explain how it works, but it works, fast.

The negative dialogue that used to run continuously through my head isn't there anymore. The way that I feel about myself has changed. I sleep better at night. I seem to be able to handle the stresses of life without falling apart. I have better impulse control.

I no longer equate sex with love and I don't seek out men for sex to make me feel better. Over the course of my life, I know I've hurt people and created a lot of damage with my destructive behavior when it comes to men, but after EMDR therapy, I feel like a totally different person.

I tried to date after my divorce, and it was a disaster. Really, I need to write a book about it one day because it was as hilarious as it was eye-opening. Once I started to get help, the way I viewed myself—and the world around me—changed. I realized that I was dating to recreate what I had already found with Ivey, with men that could never be him. And that wasn't healthy, or fair to anybody.

So, instead of urgently trying to fill the void with another man—which is what I had been doing all my life, I decided that I would give up men for awhile. No more dating and definitely no sex. What first started as kind of a challenge for myself—just to see if I could do it, turned into this beautiful journey of self-discovery.

I never realized how much of my time was consumed with chasing love. My friendships with other women have grown, and I spend more time with my son. I got a puppy, took up woodworking, and starting writing this book. I tried to learn how to garden and discovered that I hated it, but I do love to mow my yard. And, imagine my shock when I figured out that I actually enjoy being alone. Well, alone with my kid, dogs, and on the couch with Kim, watching our shows.

I don't want to be single for the rest of my life—I loved being married and being a wife, but even if I do end up alone, I know that I'm going to be just fine.

I'm no longer chained to the memories of my past and I've found freedom from the prison of my mind. The guilt and shame that has plagued me my entire life is gone. I still have a long way to go, but in many ways, I think I'm closer to being the woman I would have been if I hadn't had the childhood experiences that I did.

It was imperative to me to address this topic again in this book, even briefly, because now I'm able to write about it from the perspective of a woman that has gotten help. I implore you, if you have unresolved trauma from your past, please seek help. It's never too late. And it will change you.

18

LITERARY LAUREATE
PRESENT DAY

February 4th, 2015 is the day I found God, and the day I got clean. I wrote and completed my first memoir, *Addict Chick: Sex, Drugs & Rock 'N Roll*, during the first seven months of recovery. It was published and released exactly one year to the day that I put the dope down for the last time.

I planned to start the next book right away, fully expecting to write the story of how Cage and I reconciled and built this amazing new life together. I even thought that he could be the "Addict Dude" to my "Addict Chick." Cringy, I know. We can all be thankful that life didn't turn out that way.

At the time, losing Cage forever, especially after I ended the book the way that I did, was the worst possible scenario. That damn cliffhanger would haunt me. Almost immediately following the book's release and in all the years since, my inbox has been inundated with women asking me what happened to Cage? Did we get back together? Have I seen him? Was he clean? Everybody wanted to know what happened to him, and I couldn't answer, because I didn't know. And I couldn't start the next book because I had no idea what I would write.

Every word, paragraph, and page of the first book had come easy, but then I felt lost, unable to figure out where to go next. I know that I'm never going to be a writer like Faulkner or Kipling, and I'll never be a literary laureate and win the Nobel Peace Prize, but I love to write, and I want to be an author more than anything.

As life moved along and the years slipped by, I can't tell you how many nights I've laid awake, tossing and turning, tormented by the 'next' book. I started writing it at least twenty times, but the more time that passed, the more pressure I felt. And there was never a time that ever felt like the right time.

Until now.

I began writing *Addict Chick unCaged* in April 2020—at the beginning of the COVID-19 quarantine—just over five years from the day I got clean. So many things had happened in the in-between years that my biggest challenge was figuring out how I would write this book without it turning into the size of Tolstoy's *War and Peace*.

When I sat down to write the first page, thoughts and ideas quickly spilled out of my head and through my fingertips onto my laptop's keyboard. Rock bottom is not an easy thing to describe to people that have never experienced it, but it's completely unforgettable to those that have. It didn't take long for me to realize that this book would focus on my first year of recovery and all the obstacles I faced. Figuring out how to write about that year in the form of a story was a bit more challenging.

However, long before the ideas for this book were constructed in my mind and before the first word on the first page had been typed into this manuscript, there was a part of this story that had already been written—the ending.

Nearly a decade after it all started, and five years since I last saw him, Cage and I would finally meet again.

And I discovered that once the lights were on, I could see what was left to the imagination in the dark.

19

FULL CIRCLE

"Honey, why are you doing this?"

I stood at the kitchen counter, tossing things into my purse, but stopped and turned to face my mom. She was sitting on the couch with a cup of coffee in her hands, looking worried.

"It's important to me," I say, folding my arms and trying not to sound irritated. We've been having the same conversation repeatedly for the last few days.

"You keep saying that, but I still don't understand why." She furrows her brow, hesitating. "It's been so long, and I just don't know what you hope to get out of seeing him again."

"Mama, we've been over this. I just want to see him. I wish you would stop worrying so much. It's going to be fine." I give a reassuring smile. "You know how hard it was for me when I had to leave Texas without Cage ever seeing me clean again—it drove me crazy for years."

I take a deep breath and try my best to be patient. I understand why she is apprehensive; she will forever relate my relationship with Cage to the addiction that destroyed my life. I'm sure she imagines that ten minutes after I see him, I'll be laid up in a trap house somewhere with a needle stuck in my arm.

"What if he doesn't want to see you?" Her question verbalizes the fear that has been running through my head and freezes me in my tracks.

Cage doesn't know I'm coming. I've been too scared to call him and tell him that I tracked him down like a psychopath, and I haven't wanted to risk him saying he doesn't want to see me. After all these years, I'm just planning on showing up at his work and yelling, "Surprise!" And then hoping like hell he doesn't freak out and call the cops on me.

Finding him was a challenge; the man had gotten out of prison and disappeared off the face of the earth. I couldn't find him on any social media platforms, leading me to believe that I had just dreamed him up. Who in the world doesn't have Facebook? Unicorns and—apparently—Cage.

Good thing that within my wheelhouse of talents, I possess skills that could get me a job at the FBI. I tracked down a few people we both used to know, but they had no idea where he is—they hadn't heard from him in years. I checked the Texas Department of Corrections website and confirmed that he is not currently incarcerated. Feeling morbid, I did a Google search to see if he had been listed in any obituaries. Thankfully, the only person who popped up with his name had been seventy years old.

Continuing my quest, I scoured through piles of letters we had written to each other over the years, searching for a clue. Some were difficult to read—painful and dark. Still, I pressed on. Finally, I found mention of a possible job opportunity through one of his old high school friends.

It was a long shot, but I headed over to the company's Facebook page and started scrolling through the photos, searching for a face that I had once known as well as my own. I was about to give up when I found what I'd been looking for; in the back row of a group shot of employees stood Cage. Adrenaline shot through my body. He looked the same as I remembered—same sexy crooked smile, strong perfect jawline, and eyes that could still make my heart turn over in my chest.

I checked the date of the photo, and a surge of disappointment washed through me; the picture was over a year old. I flicked back up through the photo album, searching for another shot, but there wasn't one. I was devastated, unsure of where to go from there. I'd exhausted every possible avenue of tracking Cage down. I was only in Texas for a week to visit my family, and I was running out of time. Having decided that I needed to see him, I couldn't think of anything else.

I was about to close out of Facebook when I saw a blue button with a little white icon in the shape of a phone. I supposed I should call them, just to cross it off my list—maybe they could give me his contact information if nothing else. My thumb hovered over the button, and I clicked it before I lost my nerve.

After a few rings, my call was answered by a cheerful receptionist, and I suddenly had no idea what to say. Explaining that I was looking for an ex-boyfriend that used to work there would sound like I was a crazy stalker. She would probably hang up on me. Finally, I just asked for Cage by name.

"Cage isn't working today, but he will be back tomorrow. Would you like to leave a message, or is there something that I can help you with?"

I nearly fell off my bed. Holy. Shit. Cage still worked there—I couldn't believe it. I was so shocked that I just sat there with my mouth hanging open, not saying a word.

"Ma'am, can I take a message for him?" the receptionist asked. I could have reached through the phone and kissed her.

"No, I'll try back tomorrow, but thank you so much," I replied and disconnected the call.

It's a day later, now, and I'm leaving my worried mother behind to make the drive up to Dallas. What are the chances that Cage would still be working there? I'm guessing pretty slim; it's been like five years since he got out of prison. I can't believe my luck.

It's time, and I'm ready.

I feel a pang of uncertainty as I near the outskirts of Dallas, and my heart begins to race. Cars weave in and out of traffic, zooming past each other, all headed toward the daily grind. Once upon a time, that was my life too. It seems like a million years ago now. I was a different person back then. Even with these familiar sights around me, it's hard to imagine that this was ever my life.

Outside, the day looks perfect; the sun shines brightly from a cloudless blue sky. We're at the point in the year where you bundle up against the cold as you leave your house in the morning, but as soon as the sun is up, it's so freaking hot that you want to rip your clothes off. And this is Texas, so the humidity is thick enough that you could wear it like a set of bra and panties.

I pull my lower lip into my mouth and wonder what the hell I'm even doing here. After all this time, why have I come back? The heat inside the car intensifies, and I can smell fear coming off me in waves. Doubts tumble around in my head, and I contemplate turning around and heading back to the safety of my mama. Instead, I press my foot onto the gas and floor it right past the sign that says, "Welcome to Dallas." I turn up the volume on my radio, and Halestorm floods in as apprehension gives way to nostalgia.

I have lived between California and Texas most of my life, spending large amounts of time in both states. Even though I was born in California, I settled in Texas during my late twenties and started a life here. Politics aside, I've always felt like Texas was the epitome of America. I mean, what's more American than the Texas State Fair?

Texas is where everybody's exes live and where high-school football is considered a religion. We eat tacos from gas stations, and Buc-ee's is a national treasure. Southern hospitality is a real thing here, and every sentence ends with either "sir" or "ma'am." Our BBQ is the best, and you will be run out of the state if you try and tell us it's not. God blessed Texas, and He will judge you by how sweet your tea is—and it can never be sweet enough. You can say that you're from Texas, and there isn't a human on Earth that doesn't know where that is. The Lone Star State gave the world Willie Nelson, Mathew McConaughey, Janis Joplin, and Chuck Norris. You're welcome. It also gave us Carole Baskin, but we don't talk about that because... well... you know why. I just love America; Independence Day is my favorite holiday, and Texas is everything that feels like home to me—at least, it used to feel like home.

It's been a very long time since I was in Dallas—even longer since I lived here. Actually, the only time I lived in Dallas proper was when I lived in a trap house in Oak Cliff. Typically, most people that say they live in Dallas don't really *live* in Dallas—they live in one of the hundreds of neighboring suburbs.

In the years that I've been gone, the city has changed—grown—sprawling out in every direction. The ever-expanding skyline is still, in my well-traveled opinion, the most beautiful in the world. The small pockets of little rural towns that used to surround

Dallas now look like urbanization has spread through them, with massive shopping centers and millions of restaurants everywhere, connected by miles and miles of highway.

Even with all the expansion and development, some things never change. The roads are still wide, the buildings tall, and the ongoing road construction will forever be why nobody can make it to work on time. Affluence and wealth are stacked beside the poor and indigent, but the city keeps moving—cars, people, and life—rushing by.

Dallas is the city that celebrated with me when life was good and cried with me when it wasn't. Where I bought my first home, sent my son to kindergarten, and was surrounded by family. I can drive to any part of town without needing a GPS, and there isn't a store I haven't shopped my way through. Dallas is the place that turned me from a girl into a woman.

I pass the mall I would take Mason to when he was a baby and remember the hours I spent driving around it, trying to get him to fall asleep. I see the furniture store from which we bought his first big boy bed and the stadium where we watched his first baseball game. My heart aches for all the memories I'll never remember.

Regret burns through me when I drive beside the building where I used to work. Years of my life were spent inside those glass walls, chasing money and success, but losing sight of what should have been the most important thing in my life—being a mom. The memories flowing through me are so vivid and painful, I feel like I am living through them all over again. I can taste them in my mouth, feel them in my heartbeat, and smell them inside my mind.

Dallas, where I fell in love, had my heart crushed and my life ruined—where the line between two very different lives had been drawn—with the deep, dark, and painful chasm of my meth addiction right through the middle.

Nostalgia can be as addicting and destructive as dope. I let it carry me right into the relationship I once shared with Cage. Our love, which I thought had faded long ago, is still somehow unfinished and alive inside my head. Like the smoldering embers of a fire about to burn down the world—and all I want is to get to him.

I skirt the city and head north, relieved that the traffic has thinned out. I'm tempted to slam my foot to the floor but keep my speed just under eighty. Texas is not a state in which you want to get pulled over, even if it's just for speeding. I stay in the right lane; the exit I need isn't far, and I'm so anxious that there is a good chance I will fly right past it. With my left hand on the steering wheel, I reach into the passenger seat and pluck lipgloss from my purse, swiping it across my mouth.

I have to turn the radio off to hear the directions—an indicator that I'm getting old—and *Siri* informs me that my exit is coming up. Hitting my blinker, I veer to the right and take the ramp. I can feel the anxiety start to build inside my chest, so I roll my window down and hope that the fresh air will prevent the heart attack I'm about to have. A stop sign comes out of nowhere, and I slam onto the brakes, managing to stop the car before it careened into the intersection.

"Relax," I say, trying to calm my ass down. Taking a deep breath, I pull myself together and glance at the screen on my phone. My destination is a quarter of a mile away. I once again debate whether or not to make a u-turn and head back to mama, but the bastard behind me decides to lay on his horn—pushing me even closer to a coronary infarction.

"Relax," I say again, this time to the douchebag that obviously can't wait to see me die. I hesitate for another second, just to be a brat, and then continue through the intersection. My heart pounds so hard that I can feel it slamming between my ribs like a ping-pong ball. Anxiety climbs to full-blown panic when I turn into the parking and see the building I know Cage is currently inside.

The knowledge that—after all these years—Cage is literally on the other side of a wall is my undoing. I get the cold sweats, my stomach tightens, and now I have to poop. I can't help it; I'm a nervous pooper. And this moment goes way beyond just nervous. After five years of regrets and wondering, I'm going to finally see him again. And he is going to see me. And I have no idea what to expect or how he will react.

I park in the closest spot and recline my seat. Releasing my breath as my body falls back, I slam my eyes shut and try to get myself under control. I need to take a moment, or there's a chance I'll have an accident. It wouldn't be the worst thing that could happen. At least I would have a reason to bail since I don't have a change of clothes. Gross. Focusing on my breathing, I don't move, and my gut starts to settle down.

"Stop being a chicken shit," I mutter under my breath.

How many times have I thought of this moment—dreamed about it—especially during the first year after I got clean? Hadn't that been one of the most significant forces that had carried me through that year? The fantasy of Cage and I still in love, finding our way back to each other, and building a life together again, without drugs? But even after that dream had been crushed and broken, fate had still denied me the one thing I really wanted, even more than his love—him to see me clean again.

For years, I was haunted by the thought that the last time Cage had seen me was when I was strung out on dope. It was a nightmare that stayed inside my head, torturing me during the nights I couldn't sleep. It taunted me, and for a long time, I let it consume me.

What the hell is wrong with me? I finally have the chance to put that nightmare to bed, and here I am, cowering in my car like a coward. Who even am I right now? This isn't me. I've spent the last five years re-creating myself—I'm strong, fearless, and confident. Now, I have more balls than a tennis court.

I raise my seat, peek out the window, and scan the area. I would do a little reconnaissance and get the lay of the land before I made my grand entrance. I pray to God that Cage doesn't see me because I couldn't imagine anything worse than him seeing me huddled in my car, acting like a paranoid tweaker.

That thought is enough motivation for me to grab the handle and push the car door open. Swinging my legs out, I briefly remember the last time I did this, back when I was about to see Cage after a long absence—when he was being released from prison, and I was still in active addiction. Since then, my thighs have gotten thicker, and now I'm wearing clothes that actually cover my body. I was careful this morning when I picked out my outfit because I didn't want to look like I was trying too hard. So, I settled on a pair of jeans with a Rolling Stones t-shirt and black boots. Pretty much my standard uniform.

Taking a deep breath to steady myself, I walk carefully toward the entrance. Passing beneath a graceful sweep of trees, I reach for the heavy glass doors and push them open. I hesitate for a second—wasn't it Al Capone that said, "Once in, there is no way out?" Or something like that? I don't know why I'm suddenly thinking about a gangster, but I do know that once I cross over this threshold, there will be no going back. Biting the inside of my cheek, I fortify my resolve and step inside.

The small entryway is empty, and the silence is so heavy that it roars inside my head. To the right is a breezeway, and I force myself to walk until I'm standing in front of a reception desk. A beautiful girl with brunette hair and dark brown eyes looks up at me and smiles. I wonder if it's the same chick I spoke to yesterday. She is wearing a tight black dress that clings to her, hiding what decency demanded but leaving very little to the imagination. She is young and beautiful and exudes confidence. I like her immediately.

"May I help you?"

I stand there like an idiot and say nothing. The adrenaline and blood rushing through my body make my knees weak, and I can feel myself trembling. She looks at me and raises her eyebrow. I try to find my voice. I probably look like a crazy person.

"Yes," I say, managing to connect my racing thoughts to my mouth. "I'm here to see Cage, please."

If she responds, I don't hear it because suddenly the air is electric, and the oxygen is sucked out of the room. The pressure is massive, and the world snaps around me. Particles of light flash, and the beating of my heart sounds like an echo inside my soul.

Cage is in this room. I can sense him. I can feel him, and every part of my body catches on fire.

Across the distance, I watch as a man stops abruptly, his back to me; shoulders so broad that he could carry the weight of the entire world on them. It's Cage, and I can tell by the way he turns around that he is aware of me too. My eyes cling to him, marking time like memories across a measuring tape. He still dominates a room like nobody I've ever met, and waves of thirst build inside me, downing out every doubt and fear inside my head. I hold my breath with every agonizing inch that he turns, desperate to see the face of the man that changed my life.

When our eyes meet, the blaze between us ignites, and the

entire world goes up in flames. My mind curves into a tunnel that connects us as everything in the room disappears, leaving us alone. In this time—in this place—nothing else exists. Maybe it never did. I study Cage's beautiful face. He doesn't look shocked or surprised; it's like he's been waiting for me. And he is just as sexy as I remembered. His lower lip juts out, and the tongue that once explored every part of my body raises to the top of his mouth.

"Wind."

I can't hear it, but I can see my name drift across the distance between us, slamming into my soul. My heart shudders, my mind in complete chaos, and I almost come apart. Drawing the magic of the moment into my lungs, I inhale and hear thunder in my ears. The silver thread between us creates a magnetic force, and I feel myself being pulled towards him. Burning hot tears fall down my face before I've taken a single step. I'm breathless and weak. Cage stares at me, and his control over me plays across his face. He has the power to speak to me without saying a word, and right now, he is saying, "Come to me."

All restraint gone, I lurch toward him, my body in a race against my mind. His scent meets me halfway and washes across my body. He smells like a storm—thunder and rain—and I can feel him like a tempest inside my bones. Gravity disappears beneath my feet as Cage reaches for me and lifts me from the ground. I ache as long-forgotten memories slip through my defenses, and I remember all the moments that I had existed against his chest—my legs locked around his waist—our loved carved into the meeting of our bodies. Cage and I, together in a world made for two.

Here I am again, and the years between us disappear. It's like I never left. Nuzzled into the nape of his neck, I feel his body tremble against mine. In that instant, I recognize how powerful this moment is for us both. Cage is crying. I slide my hand behind his head and bury his face against my shoulder, hiding his tears and protecting him from the eyes of those around us. I let myself fall into him, and we stay like that for a very long time.

God, this feels so perfect, so right, that maybe this was the way it was always supposed to be. Love is a wild and mysterious thing, and perhaps this has been our fate all along. Safe in his arms, the past just melts away, disappearing from my mind.

"Wind, I missed you," he whispers, making me shiver.

"I missed you too." I hadn't realized how much until this very second, and the tears start to pool again.

"Wind, Wind, Wind," he kept repeating. "Yes, it still reminds me of you."

He inhales sharply and squeezes me one last time before letting me slide slowly down his body and onto my feet. Stealing a glance from beneath long black lashes, I stare up at him, and he throws his head back and laughs.

"What the hell are you doing here?" His eyes spark with green fire. "Damn, Wind, I can't believe you're here, standing in front of me."

"Crazy, right? It's been a long time."

He lets out another laugh, the sound conjuring up a million memories before he grabs me and pulls me against his body, his arms circling me around my waist. Dipping his head to my ear, he whispers, "And you are still beautiful."

Slipping my arms between us, I slide my hands up his chest, shamelessly checking out his body through the thin, blue dress shirt. His frame is tight and hard, still ripped with the muscles I used to trace with my fingers at night. "Jesus," I say under my breath. Leaning into me, I feel his body shift, and the heat between us builds. I consider the legal ramifications for ripping off my clothes in this very public place but then remember that my socks don't match, and neither do my bra and panties. Also, that isn't why I'm here, even if my body disagrees.

Shaking my head to clear my thoughts, I push away from him. "I needed to see you."

Concern spreads across his face. "What's wrong? Are you okay?"

"Oh, it's nothing serious. I just decided that it was finally time."

I don't need to explain; I can see that he completely understands what I mean. I suspect that he has also known that one day we would see each other again. It was inevitable. You can't end the kind of relationship we had with a phone call from prison and a letter. It has never been enough—not for me. Apparently, it hasn't been for him either.

"Let's go," he says before grabbing my hand and steering toward a bank of offices on the right side of the room. The fog has started to lift, and I notice that we aren't alone. There are people all over the place, and they're staring at us. Shit, I hope I didn't get him into trouble by showing up here and basically climbing his body like a jungle-gym. He leads me through a door and tells me that he'll be right back. He flashes me a smile before disappearing out the door.

I watch him go, staring after him in awe. Cage was wearing a business suit, and I just now noticed. I think he was even wearing a pair of black oxfords. Clearly, I must be living in some alternate universe because the Cage I know used to rock jeans and T-shirts with naked chicks on them. I don't think I ever saw him in a suit during our time together.

Lowering myself into a chair, I look around the glass-enclosed office and cannot be more shocked. On the front of the door is a freaking nameplate—this was *his* office. Damn, Cage had come up. He had done it—he got out of jail and has been leading a successful life. Isn't this what I always wanted—for him to stay clean and make it? I'm so proud of him that I almost start crying.

I scan his desk, searching for photos that might offer a clue to his life, but there aren't any. Does that mean he isn't married? What are the chances of that? After all this time and years apart, did I come back at exactly the right time?

"I still can't believe you're here, sitting in my office," Cage says, standing in the doorway, that sexy crooked smile still planted on his face.

Startled out of my fantasy, I stare at him. I thought that every part of Cage was imprinted on my memory—that he lived inside my blood—but I had forgotten about the way his sexy, smooth voice sounds when he smiles. My gaze sweeps across his face, learning it all over again. The firm set of his jaw, the cut of his cheekbones, and those entrancing eyes that could eat my soul. They travel up and down my body, making my heart race and my hands sweat.

"I can't believe I'm here either. You look great, Cage—you really do."

"Thanks. So do you. Hell, I don't even know what to say." Walking to the other side of the desk, his hand brushes across my shoulder and a tingle shoots through my body. He drops into the chair and leans back, pulling the side of his lower lip into his mouth, locking it in place with his teeth. Oh, God. He still does that, and I feel like the world has just tilted. I wasn't just gone—I was a goner.

"Have you been working here since you got out?"

"I started a few months after, so yes, pretty much."

"It looks like you've done well for yourself."

His smile grows, pride on his face. "I've done alright—kept my head down and stayed out of trouble."

"Isn't it ironic that when we met, I was the corporate businesswoman, wearing suits to work every day, and now you're the one in a suit?" I ask, laughing. "I haven't gone to an office in nearly ten years."

He burst out laughing, and it sounds husky and sexy. "That's the only thing I don't like about this job—the suit. Outside of work, I still wear the same kind of shit I always have."

"With a backward-facing hat?" I tease.

He winks at me. "Of course."

I flick a glance at his hand to see if he is wearing a ring, and he isn't. I want to ask him if he is married or has a girlfriend, but I'm scared; I don't want to hear him tell me yes. That would ruin everything. Instead, I ask him a question that I'm relatively sure I already know the answer to. Folding my hands on his desk, I lean forward.

"You've stayed clean then—all this time?"

The corner of his lip twitches. "Wind, I haven't used since the last time I got out, after that time you picked me up." His eyes bore into me, hard and unflinching. "I'm still on paper for that, but I only have a few years to go, and I'll be off parole."

I swallow hard at his bitter tone. That explains why Cage doesn't have any social media. My heart catches as memories surface, and the familiar guilt rises in my mind. Flashes of our last run together and all that I had done to make that happen beat through me. Regret crawls up my spine and lodges in my throat.

"Cage, I am sorry—I need you to know that."

Softly he says, "I hate that it happened, but I don't blame you—not anymore."

I nod, closing my eyes, but the images are there, forever

stamped with. Memories die hard, and a surge of pain shoots between us as old wounds of the heart are ripped open. I feel the air change in the room; we're not alone.

"Hey, I'm sorry to interrupt, but I have a question."

My eyes fly open, and I see the receptionist from earlier standing outside the door, looking at me. I turn my head towards Cage, and he stares back at me, amused. I raise my eyebrows, silently asking him if she is talking to me. He lets the question hang in the air, clearly enjoying my discomfort. Turning back, I face the girl.

Her gaze is still fixed on me, and she is even more beautiful than I thought. Then it hits me. Oh, my God, this was his wife—or maybe girlfriend—I know it. I look at Cage again, truly horrified, and his eyes laugh back at me. This was about to get really awkward. I turn back to the chick, and she is still smiling, confusing me even more. I shift in my seat—nervous— I have no idea what is about to happen.

"How long will you be here? I follow you on social media, and I've read your book. Do you think you could sign it for me if I run home and get it?"

My jaw drops to the floor, and my eyebrows shoot up. I didn't expect *that*. "You know who I am?"

"Of course. You're Wind, right?"

I shoot another glance at Cage, who is still laughing. "Do they know that it's you in the book?" I whisper from behind my hands.

"Yes, everybody I work with knows who you are and about your book. You kind of made me famous." His vivid green eyes twinkle. "And they also know how I screw, so thanks for that." His deep laugh fills the room.

I'm not sure what to think. I just assumed that I would be the deep dark secret Cage would keep buried—he hated my book and that I had written about our relationship. I never imagined that he would tell anybody about me, and certainly not about the book.

I look back at the chick, still standing in the doorway, and return her smile. "You don't have to go home—I have extra books in my car, so I'll just sign one of those for you."

"Really?"

"Yeah, no problem. Cage can grab it from me when I leave."

"That's great! Thank you so much!"

As the girl leaves, I turn back to face Cage. "I don't understand—how do they all know?"

Shrugging, he says, "I told one person, and then it just kind of got out."

I take a deep breath. "I hope that it didn't cause problems for you—everybody finding out about your past and the addiction like that. When I wrote the book, I didn't think about how it might affect you one day. I'm sorry."

"Wind, I've never hidden my past from anybody here. They all know that I was in prison for drugs. I'm not ashamed of that because what matters is that I'm clean now and have been for a very long time."

I'm struck by how similar our lives are—we're both clean, we own our past and the mistakes we made there, and we've survived when the odds were stacked against us. Our experiences run parallel to each other but exist miles apart.

"I'm proud of you, Wind." His voice is thick and choked with emotion. "I'm not on social media, but everybody around here keeps me updated on your life." He pauses, taking a breath. "There is something that I need to tell you. I should have said it a long time ago."

When I first met Cage, I was taken by how confident and fearless he was about everything. Even when we were on drugs together, he never seemed scared or anxious. Cage was power—he lived it, and he breathed it. But now I see vulnerability cross his face. I pull in a ragged breath, steeling myself for what is coming.

"You've apologized a million times, but never once have I told you that I was sorry." Tears begin to pool in his eyes, and a throb of agony shoots through me as they fall down his face. "After I got out of prison, I was so scared that one day I would find out you relapsed and died, and I knew that it would be my fault. You would never have gotten high and become an addict if it hadn't been for me."

I can hear the deep ache in his voice, and it slices through me. "Cage, I—."

"Wind—let me finish," he says, his voice hard and unyielding. "As the years passed and you stayed clean, I was relieved. But I've never forgotten how completely I screwed up your life—our lives. And I'm sorry—for everything. You deserved better."

I'm not about to start throwing stones because we both know that my own house is made of very cracked glass. My eyes burn. "We both screwed up, but I forgive you. You need to forgive yourself. Life happened, addiction happened, but we both made it to the other side—clean."

He smiles sadly. "I always wondered if we would still be together if none of it had ever happened—the addiction, I mean." His gaze shoots towards me, and I can see my pain mirrored in his eyes, full of regret. "I heard that you're married now—congratulations—I hope he is good to you."

He doesn't know. I'm surprised, but I don't know why—my divorce from Ivey has been painful and not something that I have blasted across social media.

"Actually, we divorced a few months ago," I say quietly. Speaking the words out loud unleashes a fresh wave of anguish through me, and I almost double over. I don't want to think about Ivey, not right now, and I try to push the image of his face out of my mind. Our marriage is over—I'm free to do what I want, go where I want, and see who I want—but somehow, being here with Cage feels like a betrayal to Ivey.

"Really?" He asks, sounding startled, and his voice brings me back to the moment.

"Yeah. How about you—are you married yet?"

He shakes his head. "Not married, but I have a girlfriend. We've been together since I got out."

"Are you happy?"

"Mostly—we have good days and bad, but she has stuck by me, and you know how important loyalty is to me." His focused stare loudly speaks the words he doesn't say.

I press my lips together, bow my head in shame, and hold my breath as a cacophony of thoughts race through my head. He was reminding me that I betrayed him in unforgettable ways. I left him in prison, cutting him off without a word. It doesn't matter that I had done it because he cheated on me. We both know that leaving him wondering and worried about my safety—with no way to find out if I was okay—wasn't the behavior of a chick that was down for her man.

The ride or die mentality—the root of our relationship. There wasn't anything I wasn't willing to put up with, nothing I wouldn't do, as long as Cage loved me. I accepted the unacceptable, did the unimaginable, but then, I did the unforgivable. Sick and controlled by addiction, I let another man take my body. For Cage, that was inexcusable.

But the girl that had once granted Cage blind devotion and utter obedience no longer exists. I killed her a long time ago. I'm not that woman anymore, and I never will be again. Not for Cage or any other man.

Now, it's impossible to cage the wind.

My head shoots up, and I return his unrelenting gaze with one of my own. The intensity fires away between us, threatening to erupt. Again, I study him, drawing every part of him back into my soul. For nearly a decade, I have chased this man—chased him in love and rushed after him into addiction. I have hunted him through hate and worshiped him in bed. He was once everything I ever wanted, and our passion consumed and destroyed me. I have spent hours of my life fantasizing that we would one day find our way back to each other because our love could never die.

We watch each other, both struggling with the war being waged inside our heads, and the silence grows between us. I start thinking about Ivey, comparing him to Cage—I can't help it. From the second I met Ivey, fell in love, and married him, I rarely thought of Cage at all. If I hadn't written a book about our lives together, I don't think I would be sitting here now.

I feel a twinge of regret as I finally understand. Who I am—who Cage is—those people don't match, not anymore. And they never will again. We've become different people, and our love story ended a long time ago. I'm not here to cut open the scars that have long since healed— that isn't why I came. No, I came to say goodbye for the last time—it just took a little longer for my heart to catch up with what my mind already knew. By his face, Cage knows it too.

"Cage, I'm glad that you're doing good. It's the only thing I ever wanted for you—to be clean and have a happy life." I smile at him, my eyes dry. "I have to head out." I decide on the spot that I'm going back to say goodbye to my mom and family, but I'm leaving the next day to get back to Mason in Kentucky—where I belong.

Cage stands up, comes around the desk, reaches for my hand, and pulls me to my feet. "I'm not worried about you—not anymore. You're going to make it." Smiling, he pulls me into his arms, and I know that coming here was the right thing to do.

There is no more hate or bitterness, and all the resentments are gone. I didn't have to wonder anymore—all of my unanswered questions have been answered. Cage has finally seen me clean, putting to rest the regret that has been following me around for the last five years.

It was time to cross the bridge between Cage and I—and light that bitch on fire.

Later, as Dallas disappears behind me, I know that I will never live here again. Everything in life has a beginning and an ending, and I've made peace with the life I once had in this city. I suppose my only regret is that it took me so long to find it—that, and letting so much of my past crawl with me into the future.

Apprehension fills me as the authentic part of me demands that I get honest with myself. While I may have finally reconciled my past with Cage, I have another part of my life that's breaking me apart—the one I destroyed with Ivey. Suddenly, all I want is to see the man that wasn't my husband anymore, crawl into his lap, and feel his strong fisherman arms around my body. Ivey feels like home, even now, and that makes me ache.

The partners I became with Cage and Ivey were two completely different women, and I screwed up both of them.

With Cage, I had completely lost myself in every way, becoming somebody that I can't imagine ever being. I was meek, insecure, and did so many things for which I'm ashamed. I had no pride or self-esteem, and I didn't see value in who I was. I worshipped him, letting the rest of my life fall apart, and that started long before we began using dope together. I barely spent any time with Mason. I neglected my career, destroyed friendships, and pushed away my family—always preferring to spend my time with Cage over anybody else. Our relationship had been explosive and violent, and still, I stayed.

The crazy wild sex I wrote about in the book wasn't healthy, and it wasn't as hot as I made it sound. You can do a lot with adverbs and adjectives when you're living a fantasy. I watched Cage bang other women and pretended that it was okay because I wanted to be that open-minded chick that I believed all men want—especially men like Cage. I love women, but I've never desired them sexually. Yet, I went to bed with them and pretended to love it while Cage watched. Still, I stayed.

I had been against drugs my entire life but gratefully stuck out my arm for a needle full of meth just so that I could keep being with Cage. In the dope game, we became even more destructive and evil together. I lost every part of myself. Still, I stayed.

He went to prison, addiction tore us apart, and then we both got clean. In my head, I stayed.

Then I met Ivey and realized that what I thought was love with Cage wasn't even close. There isn't one comparison I could ever make between my relationship with Cage and the one I found with Ivey. Ivey was the godly man that I had been praying for every night before I went to sleep. The connection between us was instant and mutual. He became my best friend overnight, and I had never felt safer. The first time we made love was on our wedding night, and married sex is the hottest sex I've ever had.

Ivey would die before he ever hurt me, and there isn't a world that exists where he would stick a needle in my arm. He treated me with respect and love. Ivey prayed for me every night—and there is nothing more beautiful than that. He wasn't good at showing his emotions, but if there is anything I would bet my life on, it's that I know he loved me deeply.

But I was so hell-bent on never losing myself again that I allowed no grace for even the smallest mistakes. Marriage is hard, even when you love each other, but instead of working through our issues, I just bounced. Many of those issues came from my insecurities. No matter how hard he tried or what he said, I could never believe that he wasn't cheating on me. He would never do that, but that wasn't something I believed until it was too late. And now I have to live with that too.

Happiness and balance must lay between the extremes of the women I became with Cage and Ivey. On one side, I surrendered myself completely, becoming a doormat. On the other, I was too dominant—an unforgiving bitch that took no shit. Both sides were equally destructive, and neither would give me the one thing that I want above all else—love—and a relationship that I don't screw up.

Tears blaze a trail of regret down my face, and the ache inside my chest burned like fire. I shouldn't feel like this— I have a great life, and I'm truly blessed. My son is healthy, and I have a fantastic family. I've found professional success again and am living my dream as an author. I've purchased a home and finally gotten my shit together financially. I'm clean, I have the support of my Addict Chick family, and I have enduring friendships with women that I adore.

I have so much; so many good things have happened for me, and that should be enough. I mean, why do I feel like I deserve all of that and love too? Maybe it's supposed to be this way; God's plan and all that.

Sometime over the past few hours, the sun had dropped low in the sky, and the moon is about to put it to bed. I look out the window and wonder what I'm getting wrong in this thing called life. There is a hole inside my chest that seems to grow bigger with every passing day. Despite all the gifts in my life, why do I feel like something is missing?

When I see the bright star shoot across the big Texas sky, I think I know.

20

MANTEO, NORTH CAROLINA—2016

The first time I saw her was in a coffee shop in the Outer Banks of North Carolina. I was there visiting my future husband, Ivey, and had a panic attack when I realized that there wasn't a Starbucks nearby. He talked me into trying a local place called the Front Porch Café, and I agreed, hoping that I wouldn't be forced to call off our engagement due to my obsession with iced coffee.

I noticed her the second we walked in, and my heart sank. She was standing in line, and all I could see was her back. Immediately, I knew that I was going to hate this chick. Thick, blond hair cascaded like waves of golden sunshine down her back, and it was her real hair too, not extensions. Sorcery. Despite the modest black leggings and long t-shirt she was wearing, you could tell that she had a killer body. I remember thinking that if I had a body like hers, I would be walking around half-naked.

She had a blond baby girl perched high onto her left hip, and as we walked to stand behind them, the toddler turned to look at us. She was gorgeous, with huge blue eyes and a perfectly pink rosebud mouth, confirming what I already suspected: a child this beautiful could only come from a mom that was equally as stunning. The kid stared at us, and I swear, I saw her eyes narrow at me like she knew I was judging her mother. I thought about sticking my tongue out at her, but being an adult, I decided against it.

I stood there, feeling threatened by a woman I didn't know and whose face I hadn't even seen. Heart pounding, I wished that Ivey was blind in the same breath that I begged God to let this woman just disappear. Instead, she suddenly turned around and looked right at us, and I begged Him to let me be the one to disappear—and, of course, take Ivey with me because no woman in her right mind would leave her man alone in a room with a woman that looked like her.

I am not exaggerating—she looked exactly how I imagined angels in heaven look, except she was missing the white feather wings—though I wouldn't have been surprised to see them sticking out of her back. Long black lashes framed soulful blue eyes that rested on cheekbones so high and perfect that they should be used for facial filler advertisements. She wasn't wearing any makeup, and she didn't need any. It's not natural or fair for a woman to roll out of bed and look like this without the help of concealer. Obviously, this chick had been blessed. Relief flooded me when I realized that it was tourist season in the Outer Banks, so she likely wasn't even from here. In a few moments, she would be gone, off the island, and I wouldn't have to worry about her ever again.

The first word out of her mouth dissuaded me from that notion.

"Ivey," she said, her melodic voice carrying my fiancé's name from her mouth right into the deep insecurity growing inside my chest. She wasn't a tourist; she was local. And she knew Ivey. And now I was going to have to burn down an entire island. Her gaze found mine, and the smile that lit up her face was so perfect that I wanted to hate her even more, but there was something about her that made it impossible.

"I saw on Facebook that you're engaged," she said, beaming. "Congratulations! I'm so happy for you both," Shifting the baby that was still looking pointedly at me to her other hip, she stuck out her hand and said, "I'm Casey."

Great, now I had a first name with which to launch a full-scale social media investigation. Taking a ragged breath, I raised my hand to meet hers. "Hey, I'm Amanda," I said, thankful that my voice didn't shake.

I'm not often intimidated by other women; I learned long ago that resenting a woman for having something you don't or the way they look is the behavior of the kind of woman that I strive *not* to be. There is room for all of us in this world, and I want every chick to make it, but I was having a hard time imagining my soon-to-be husband living right down the street from this woman.

She laughed deep, throaty, and loud—a sound that didn't seem to fit her but somehow made her even more endearing. "I know who you are—I follow your Addict Chick page on Facebook." Turning to look at Ivey, she said, "I had no idea that you knew her."

My silent fisherman just nodded his head, making me roll my eyes. Why do you need words when a shrug will do?

The little spawn in her arms started to wiggle, and I watched as Casey popped her back up on her hip before grabbing the coffee off the counter and gliding toward us in one fluid motion. She looked like a pro.

"I have to run, but I'm so happy that you found each other. I'll be praying for you and your marriage," she said before walking out the door.

"Okay, beautiful, crazy lady," I whispered under my breath. Pray for us—who says stuff like that?

I had no idea that morning that Casey would end up being the other half of my soul, the most constant thing in my life, and my best friend. One day when I'm at the end of my life, I will look back on my journey and see so many ways that God showed up for me; all the pivotal moments that altered my direction in life, and the people that profoundly affected the woman I became. Casey and our Christ-centered friendship will be one of them.

Casey grew up in the small fishing village of Wanchese, North Carolina, which is located on the south end of Roanoke Island in the Outer Banks. It's also where Ivey was born and raised and where I lived when we were married. I've traveled all around the world and have never been anywhere like Wanchese. The descendants of the same families that settled the island still live there. The men head out to sea to fish, the women wait for them to come home, and everybody lives within six square miles of each other.

I still think it's crazy that God made us best friends. Casey is a stay-at-home mom with four kids. Yes, four little humans—and three of them are girls. I get heartburn every time I think about it. I mean, I like my kid and everything, but my goal has always been to keep him alive until I can send him off to college. Casey was born to be a mom. She is a devoted wife to her fisherman husband, Brook. I loved being a wife, but I had a hard time when my preacher brother-in-law included that part about obeying your husband in our vows.

She is living the life she always wanted, and even though I know God knew better than to give me a life like that, sometimes I envy her for the peace and contentment she has. She even knows how to survive without a Target nearby.

The next time I saw Casey was when Ivey and I were attending church on Sunday, sometime after we had gotten married. It was the church that Ivey had been raised in, his father had been raised in, and I'm pretty sure his grandfather too. They have a family pew and everything. We were standing up for the music part of the service, which I know most people love, but I wasn't a big fan. The only lyrics I know are from rock 'n roll songs, and I can't sing anyway. Also, it lasts forever, and my feet always hurt.

I was wondering if I could slip my shoes off without God seeing me when Casey came rushing up the aisle, same cherub-looking baby with the judgy eyes planted on her hip, and two other kids trailing behind her. I watched as they headed to the front and piled into their family pew. My mouth dropped open when, with the baby still on her hip, she tossed her hand into the air, bowed her head, and started getting down with Jesus. I could tell she loved the Lord and wasn't scared for the world to know. I didn't grow up in the Church or with God, so I wondered if she was a religious zealot or something.

About a month later, I attended a Bible study at that very same church. My mother-in-law, Linda, was the teacher. I know many people don't like their mothers-in-law very much, but I adored mine. She was good to me and a strong Christian woman that I admire very much. She had even read my first book and *still* let her son marry me. She never came right out and said it, but I know that she had started that Bible study for me. She wanted me to have a relationship with God, but I didn't even understand how the chapters in the Bible worked.

When I walked into the church that night, Casey was there, looking just as beautiful as the last two times I had seen her.

Strangely, the child that I had assumed was permanently attached to her was missing.

We hadn't been sitting there for more than five minutes when she looked at me and said, "We have the same tattoo."

Glancing down at my fully tattooed arm, I said, "Which one?"

"We have the same Bible verse."

I didn't need to ask what verse she was talking about because I only had one—Psalm 46:5.

Slowly, I looked at her and said, "God is within her, she will not fall."

Nodding excitedly, she smiled at me, and I smiled back. And in an instant, our friendship began. God knew what he was doing when He brought her into my life. She was grace and love and had a light that burned inside her.

With Casey, there is not one single thought, secret, doubt, or worry that I haven't shared with her. I trust her explicitly. There is comfort for me in knowing that she will always be there; it settles me. She is loyal and supportive, and despite how far I may wander away from God, she never gives up on me.

I've never had a friend that prayed for me. Like, she puts her hand on my head and prays. She is good at it too. She sends me text messages all the time to remind me that Jesus loves me. When I cry, she quotes Bible verses to me. Every problem I have, her answer is always God. When my life is going great, she reminds me that it is because of God. Her faith and relationship with Jesus are humbling.

As my marriage was falling apart and I was contemplating leaving, Casey was the only person in my life that encouraged me to stay and work it out. In a loving and real way, she got angry and told me that you don't give up on your marriage or your husband, no matter what. You stay, and you work it out. She reminded me that God should be first in a marriage, then each other, then our children, and then... I don't remember the rest, but it is supposed to be in that order. Ivey and I were doing it backward, and instead of fighting for my marriage, I walked away.

When I left, she handed me two books and told me that I needed to open one every day and just read a page. It didn't matter which because God would guide me. The first book was a journal from 2015 that covered a full year of her life. There were Bible verses, her thoughts during that year, and love letters to her husband. The second was her personal Bible, cover ragged and torn; every inch covered in notes and highlighted text. Both were intimate and personal—precious gifts from the heart of my best friend.

I never opened either; I just kept them on my bedside table where they have been collecting dust for over a year. Earlier in the book, I mentioned that I began to write *Addict Chick unCaged* in April 2020, at the beginning of the COVID-19 pandemic. But the book I started writing in April isn't the same book you're reading right now. Essentially, while the world has been falling apart and I've been confined to my house, I've written two books. While both versions of the book were focused on my first year of recovery, the way I told the story was entirely different. And the difference between the two is Casey and conviction.

The day I got clean is the same day that I was saved—February 4th, 2015. I've done a lot of work to stay clean and build a new life, but I haven't done anything to honor God or build a relationship with Him. I've gone to church a handful of times but never made an effort to get involved in any way. I have Bibles that I never open and Christian books that I've never read. I've been gifted this unbelievable platform that reaches millions of people every month, and I have never used it for the glory of God. I'll write a quote here and there about the power of prayer, but I rarely pray. I've been a Christian for five years, but you probably wouldn't know it by the way that I live my life. I'm bold, but not when it comes to speaking about God—I'm scared that I'll say everything the world doesn't want to hear.

I see people that get saved, and it's like the Holy Spirit just dove right inside of them with a road map. They are so on fire for God, throwing out scripture and Bible verses like they have it all memorized. The only verse I know by heart is the one that is tattooed on my arm. I have this friend, Heidi Davis, and she is a newer Christian than I am, but she is out there fearlessly talking about God. She has changed every part of her life to serve God. Like, she doesn't even celebrate Halloween, and I'm over here trying to find a costume that makes my butt look good.

If you've read *Addict Chick: Sex, Drugs & Rock 'N Roll*, you know that the entire book is filled with graphic sex. While I don't regret writing it because I can't go back and change what was— it did damage many parts of my life. Especially in relationships and the perception of who I was as a woman. As a writer, I left the impression that I write books about sex, and because SDRR was overwhelmingly successful, when I sat down back in April and started *unCaged*, I continued to be that writer. Unnecessarily descriptive sex and filthy language—I hated every page of it. The more I wrote and the further I got into it, the more I wanted to quit. I didn't want to write like that anymore, but I felt like if I didn't, then nobody would read it, and those that did would hate it.

One afternoon, I was sitting in front of my computer, ready to throw in the towel and never write again, and Casey called me. It was strange because we text nearly every day but rarely talk on the phone.

"God laid it on my heart that I needed to call you—are you okay?"

Immediately, I started to cry. "No, nothing is okay. I don't want to write about sex anymore," I told her through my ugly crying.

"Then don't."

"But sex is what sells, right? Isn't that what I always say? If I don't write about sex, nobody is going to buy it, and the book will be a flop."

Casey hesitated, and I knew that she was probably praying for the right words to give me. "Why do you think you're struggling with this? Because God is convicting you and putting revival in your heart." She sounded so excited, but I didn't want to talk about God; I wanted her to tell me something that made me feel better. God stuff always sounded like a bunch of hard work, and writing a book is hard enough. But Casey was on a roll.

"Do you want to help people, make a difference, and change hearts? Or do you want to sell books? Are you going to let the influence of the world decide what you should write, or are you going to surrender to the will of God?" And then she was crying too. "You have the spirit of God inside of you, in your heart, and He is prompting you to do one thing. If you listen to Him, He will free you in a million ways." She spoke so quickly and adamantly that I was worried she was having an asthma attack or something.

"Casey, I love you, but I don't know what I'm going to do. I don't want to write a book about sex, but I honestly don't think I'm a good enough writer to write a book without it. I mean, what would I even write about?"

"Pick up the Bible or the journal I gave you and randomly open a page and read it to me. Right now."

"Case—"

"Please?"

I reached over and grabbed the journal that has never been opened. The first page I opened to was just a drawing of a cross on a mountain. So, I flipped through it and noticed the dates neatly written at the top.

"You have perfect handwriting," I tell her. "These are all from 2015—I'm going to see what you wrote on February fourth—my clean date."

"Thanks, and that's a good place to start."

I thumbed through the pages toward the front and found the entry. I read the first few lines and almost hung up on her, totally freaked out.

Casey broke the silence after some time. "What does it say?"

I decided that I should buy a lottery ticket after we hang up. "It says 'Exodus 20:6' at the top, and right below that, it says, 'but I lavish unfailing love for a thousand generations on those who love me and obey my commandments.' And then it says, 'A root cause of deception is hearing the word of God and not doing it.'"

"Anything else?"

"Yeah, you drew a little heart and wrote, 'Be a doer of his word' and 'People need to see God in you.'"

I can see God in so many parts of my life, and I can see the moments I missed His message. He was right there, and I can't explain how I missed it or why. Maybe I just wasn't ready. I honestly don't know, but there was no missing His message right now; He was coming through loud and clear.

"Humans are careless with timing, but God isn't—his timing is perfect." I could hear her smile, and I had never been more thankful in my entire life. "Now, go write your book and pray that you will always remember who you are, what you're called to do, and where you're going to spend eternity. I love you."

"Thank you, Case—I love you almost as much as Jesus."

"Almost," she laughed, before hanging up.

My true surrender came, and I fell into the Holy Spirit. I went back through my manuscript and ripped it apart. I deleted every page and paragraph that included sex that I had purposely written with the intent to sell more books. I struggled with leaving in the chapter about dope sex but felt like I needed to be honest about what sex on drugs was actually like. I'm not sure if I did the right thing, but I did pray about it. God didn't tell me yes or no; at least I don't think he did. However, taking Casey's advice, I randomly opened her Bible looking for answers and ended up in the book of Leviticus. I'm not sure what I read, but I'm going to need somebody to explain why Moses was putting blood and kidneys in baskets of bread. I didn't find anything that said, *"Please take out the dope sex chapter, thanks. Love, God,"* so I cleaned it up, and I'm rolling with it.

I wrote a brand new book in six weeks. I know I probably didn't do the best job exemplifying a woman of God, but let's all just appreciate that I left out tutorials on women's self-gratification. I got saved, but I did not get perfect.

I used the search function to find all two-hundred plus instances that I used the F-word and removed *most* of them. But, I will not stop saying 'badass' because the word 'ass' appears in the Bible eighty-seven times. I know I still curse more than I should, but I'm trying to clean up my language. Nonetheless, there is a one-hundred percent chance that I'll continue to drop the F-word on occasions where no other word will do. Like when I cut wood and haven't measured correctly.

I know that by claiming my place as the daughter of Christ, I will have to get into my Bible every day and try to live a life that glorifies God. I'm going to make a lot of mistakes. I'm not ready to give up Halloween, but I will dress up as a fully-covered pumpkin next year. I don't think I'll ever be jumping on Facebook Live to talk about scripture, but I will be more thoughtful and purposeful about what I write. I'm not ready to give up rock 'n roll and secular music, but I will start listening to Jesus' music too.

Writing this book has been the most difficult, humbling, and powerful experience of my life. I've drawn closer to God, and I feel different—lighter, somehow. It's strange; I look back now and see all the painful moments that led to the most beautiful. Every bad choice and sound decision, every path I've traveled—they all add up to a collection of memories that have turned into the story of my life.

And I am grateful for every season.

> "For the weariest day, may Christ be your stay.
> For the darkest night, may Christ be your light.
> For your weakest hour, may Christ be your power.
> For each moment you fall, may Christ be your all."
>
> — CASEY GALLOP STOWE

21

BADASS CHICKS

*Y*ou are the women that motivate me to work hard, be bold, and go after every damn thing they said I could never have. You are the chicks that have supported me, loved me, and made me laugh. You've taught me the importance of female friendships and inspired me in a million different ways—some of you probably don't even know it. This chapter is in thanks to all of you. God Bless.

Mom, you are my best friend, my inspiration, and the reason I spend all my money at Lowes. Thank you for loving me when I'm unlovable, kicking my ass when I need it, and for making me laugh when you do your poop walk. My love for reading is a gift from you, but you probably shouldn't have let me read Jackie Collins and Stephen King when I was only seven. Thank you—for everything—except for my slow metabolism. I love you, mama. **Courtney Caley,** my beautiful niece, I wish you had known your dad—he would have been so proud of you. I will always root for you and play with sloths and leopards with you. **Diane Giannoni,**

you're my second mama and a saint for letting me live with you during my high school years. I love you, Aunt Dena. **Dulce Giannoni**, you are one of the smartest and strongest women I know. Thank you for editing the book jacket for *unCaged*. **Joyce Appleford**, my greatest wish is that I age as beautifully as you. Bless you, for being the matriarch of our crazy family.

Linda Daniels writing about you made me cry—I miss having you for a mother-in-law. Thank you for welcoming me into your family—I still wish I had stayed. **Melissa Bryan**, you're the crazy Aunt that always makes me laugh and the first person to buy anything I'm selling. **Peyton Elizabeth Mead**, I couldn't ask for a better sister-in-law—my brother is lucky to have you. You're beautiful, smart, and I adore you. **Susan Bryant**, you will always be my sister—I miss you taking care of me. **Susan Meredith**, thank you for loving Mason like your own and being such an amazing co-mom with me. **Teresa Nulty**, cousin, friend, and confidant—I admire you. **Vanessa Willman**, I wanted a baby sister so bad, and when I finally got you, you pulled my hair. I love you, and I'm proud of you and the life you've built. I know dad is smoking a joint, drinking a beer, and looking down on us—smiling—he always said that he never had to worry about his daughters. The boys, though...

Sawyer Elaine Elizabeth Willman, you are too young to read this now, but I hope one day you will. I want you to know that you can grow up and be anything you want—your dreams are important, so follow them. Steer your own ship, and never compare yourself to anybody. That guy you think you can't live without? You can. Promise. Nobody will ever love you like your mom. Life passes by quickly, so enjoy every moment. Don't do drugs—ever. Trust your intuition. Love God with all of your heart; He will never leave you. You are magic—I cannot wait to watch your journey.

Amanda Jane Jones, 2.4.2015. **Amy Patrice Bowen,** may we always laugh at Saul Kane. **Anne Moreland Swann,** thank you for freezing my face in time and letting my family romp around on your farm. **Becki Holcomb,** I'm so glad you're in my life and that you can't arrest me anymore because I don't do drugs. #Stalkermom. **Brandi Lee Montagne,** thank you for staying up all night to be the first to buy unCaged. **Brandi Miller,** may I always be the William to your Penny Lane—Rock 'N Roll Forever. **Cali Estes,** you're a badass and the mean bitch I need in my life, but I hope you come down with trypophobia.

Casey Gallop Stowe, the next book I'm publishing, will be yours. We're calling it "Love letters to my husband and God." I love you and your kids, and there isn't anything I wouldn't do for any of you. Except, change diapers. **Corey Turner,** from the OBX to KY, I will always be your first, and you will always be a friend that I know I can trust. **Heatha Piasecki,** I love your haht and every word that you speak that ends in the letter 'R'. **Heidi Davis | Jesus Chick.** I thank God for you.

Jennifer Gimenez, thank you for writing the foreword for *unCaged* and for making Tim Ryan get a new haircut—he still isn't as hot as you, but we will all keep praying. **Jessica Glover,** thirty-plus years of friendship, and you have never been on time for anything, but I'll always wait for you. **June Dooley,** for running our social media empire with an iron fist so nobody will be mad at me—I couldn't handle a million-plus people without you. **Kaelan Lanie,** I think you are incredible and have the most beautiful soul.

Kimberly Poole, isn't it crazy that in thirty-two years, we've never had a fight—and we live together? Do you think we grew up to be addicts because we used to cheat in Senor's Spanish class? When will Lucifer be back on? Why did we not die in the groves of Clovis, CA? Do you think think Jax Teller is still alive? Why aren't our pictures on the wall in Graeters? How did we survive a semester of zero period for FBLA? I have questions. **Kimmy Assalone,** I've never met anybody like you, and you will forever be one of my favorite humans. **Krista Turner,** you remind me of myself, so I know you're going to do badass things. **Lorelie Rozzano,** I'm a huge fan of your writing, your books, and you. Thank you for writing a blurb for *unCaged*. **Lynn Connolly,** Pizza, Shoes, Closet, Forever.

Mel Serenity & Carolyn Winokur, for the fire ass memes that I don't have the guts to post on my own page. **Monica Beltran Urzua,** miles separate us, but millions of memories connect us. **Nicole Corso,** you're the mom to the first baby ever born into Addict ChickS, so you and **Mace** will always be my heart. **Ranada Riley,** you introduced me to beer cheese and fed me more often than you know during the writing of this book. **Sharen Etheridge,** thank you for giving me, Casey. **Sonja Scarborough,** your faith, loyalty, and fierceness for standing up for what you believe in, are just a few of the things I love about you. **Susan Julie,** BRAVO BITCHES.

Tajuana Mitchell, you are the only person I follow on TikTok. Thank you for the best conversations, Tony Evans podcasts, and my magical lashes. **Tammy Harris,** for taking me in, never stealing from me and being in my life on this side of the game. **Tessa Johnston,** for being an early reader for unCaged, for your friendship, and for all you do. **Tessa Bare,** you have been rockin' with me from day one, and your love and support mean more than you know. Tell **Jaz** that I love her too! **Whitney Hundley Mayer, Susan Haughaboo Ledford &Amy Haughaboo Hines,** thanks for the warm welcome to Chilesburg even though I don't live on the popular kid street.

To the women in **"A Mother's Hope,"** and to every mom with an addicted child, I see you, ache for you, and pray for you every day. Never give up hope. I love you all.

THE BADASS CHICK IN *ME* HONORS THE BADASS CHICK IN *YOU*.

ALAINA COMBS, AUTUMN CHANDLIER PITT, AUDRA MEADS SHACKLEFORD, AVALON LIVESEY, BRANDI PETERSON, BRENDA THACKER, MARILEE BRIDGET THOMAS, ABBY PARSONS, ALECHIA ANN TREECE, ALECIA HUFF, ALEX MIDDLETON, ALEXANDRA GIFFORD, ALEXANDRIA CONCHA, ALICIA ANN BORDERS, ALICIA FAUGHT, ALICIA WILSON-GARCIA, ALISHA MENEGAY, ALLY RUGE, AMANDA HENDRICKS, AMANDA K. EARLING, AMANDA KAPPES, AMBER BODNER GRIFFITH, AMBER FIFE, AMY JESSE, AMY MORROW, ANDREA VENNER BRAZIL, ANGIE RICHARDSON, HOPKINS, ANIKA COOPER, ANNEMARIE HORN, APRIL HIGGINS, APRIL LYNN PERKINS, ASHLEY BREWER, ASHLEY DUNN, ASHLEY ELLENDER, ASHLEY JACOBS, ASHLEY KING FOWLER, ASHLEY SANCHEZ, ASHLEY STEPHENS, ASHLEY WARDEN, BRANDY KING, ASHLEY WHITTON, AUTUMN DAWN HERD, AUTUMN LOCASCIO, AYSE SELMAN, BECKY RUTHERFORD, BETH VICE, BRANDI MELLON, BRENDA THACKER, BRITTANY JOHNSON, BRITTANY WILLIAMS, BROOKE GODWIN, BROOKE GOEKEN, BROOKE TAYLOR, BUFFY MCDONALD, CAMI SOTELO, CANDICE NEWSOM, CARAH ROSS, CASSIE ROY, CATHERINE HARBERT, CATHERINE MORRIS, CATHY GOMEZ, CATRINA BURTNER, CEARA RENEE KAMLA, CHARITY DAWN, CHASTITY LYNNAE KESSLER, CHELSI HUFFMAN, CHERYL MATHESON ROSE, CHRIS KELLY, CHRISTIE O'NEILL, CHRISTINA ODOM, CHRISTINA VASQUEZ, CORI BAIZA, COURTNEY KIRLIN, CRYSTAL GEGENHEIMER, CYNTHIA CRAIG, CYNTHIA SMOOT, DANIELLE SANTOS, DE BOSWELL, DEBBIE GALLOP, DEBBI HERR, DEBBI WILLMAN, DENISE MUCCI, DEVON ZANARAS, DIANE KOLB, DIANNA HEAD, DONNA CLODFELTER, DONYELLE

Woods, Eileen Lester Davies, Emily Weesner, Emma Fogle, Erica Rose, Erin Quinlan, Eva McFarlin, Evelyn McCann, Gail Mayfield, Garilynn White Kirk, Gina Cain, Gina Kissam, Gwen Gabrielli, Hayley Mulder, Heather Annette Angle, Heather Carter Daniels, Heather Moore, Heather Paul, Heather Siomiak, Holley Kaye, Jaime Stockton, Jamie Bohanon Hancock, Jamie Brown, Jammie Jones, Jan Fogle, Janet Talbot, Janet Lewis Majors, Janie Estrada, Jaye Petty, Jayme Chamberlin, Jenn Zwickel, Jennifer Daniels, Jennifer Elfstrom, Jennifer Lee Watkins, Jennifer Mangini, Jennifer McCann, Jennifer Zimmerman Oliver, Jessica Lemp, Jessie Ballor, Jessika Haley Whiteside, Jessica Renner, Jill Amaya, Jill Hill, Julie Abbott, July Clark, Julieann Beaulieu, Julynn Trota, June Talley, Kaitlyn McCurday, Katelyn Jade Terry, Katelynn Zimmerle, Kathy Lentz Johnson, Kathy Underwood Garrison, Katie Grady-Gangwer, Katie Moore Gibson, Katie Marriott, Katie OMalley, Katina Wiseman, Katrice Jackson, Katy Patton, Kayla Bates, Kayla Hill, Kaylee Moreno, Kayleen Denise Cash, Kelly Baummer, Kelly Maureen Foreback, Keondra Moore, Kerri Edgar, Kim Korbel Davenport, Kim Ryan-Schaarschmidt, Kimberly Durham, Kimberly Herren-Liles, Kimberly Thompson, Kristen Marcotte, Kristen Turner, Kristi Gabriel, Kristina Miller, Kyna Arnold, Laken Rheanna Collins, Lana Beacham, Lane Beach, Lara Ann Frazier, Larra Dunklin Selman, Latisha Stokley, Laura Stewart, Lauren Mattiacci, Lauren Ryan, Leah Cortes, Leanne Greer, Leslie Mills, Lexi Coyle, Lillian Trevathan, Linda Drake, Linda Hitch Hammond, Lindsey Rozell, Lisa Vincent, Lisa Ratliff, Livvy Jamison, London Nicole Dorsey, Lorelie Rozzano, Lori Godwin, Lori Wolf, Lynn DeLaigle Jarman, Maghan McClung, Makenzie Rozell, Mandy Bays,

AMANDA MEREDITH

Margaret Cotton, Meghan White, Melinda Keith, Melissa Lee Matos, Melissa Wolfe, Michelle McGuffog, Missy Matthews, Misty Airheart Weatherly, Monica Comeaux Cradeur, Myra Meade, Nancy Cheaves, Nicole Edwards, Nicole Klassen, Nitya Sivakumar, Pam Herwig-Kirby, Nya Nulty, Pat Howard Gibbs, Patricia Gonzalez, Paula Bailey, Paula Holman, Paula Sipe, Pauline Thomas, Penny Stone, Phyllis Livesey, Rachael Piotini, Rachel Savage, Rachel Tishara Stacy, Rachel Trentor, Rae Whalley, Renasha Crask, Rira Mccowan, Ro-Ro Harrison-Welborn, Samantha Gonzalez, Sandy Badner, Sara Chiarello, Sara Clark Davis, Sara Hollar, Sarah Klepfer, Shanna Johnson, Shannon Abernathy, Shannon Fielder, Shannon Francisco, Shannon Stewart, Sharon Spencer, Shay Walters, Shelby Elaine, Shelby Jo Stewart, Shelly Brown, Shelly Renee, Shona Taylor, Sierra Temple, Tami Hall, Tami Sterner Barthol, Tammy Brooks, Tara Flerchinger, Tara Parisi Silva, Teresa Gallop, Terry Bentley Hill, Tiara Caudill, Tiffany Daniels Ivey, Tiffany Hendra, Tiffany Montanye, Tiffany Roberts, Tina Loper, Tina Smith, Tina Warner, Tish Chlad, Toni Sears, Tori Love Peters, Torrie S. Pugh, Tracie L Costner, Tracy Daddio, Tracy Manion, Tracy Spencer, Tracy Ward, Tricia Cary, Trish Jenkins, Trisha Chappel, Valerie Eagen Hiatt, Vera Berenyi Bates, Victoria Conklin.

Thank you for being part of my journey.

I hope you loved the book!
Please don't forget to throw up a
quick review wherever you bought it.

ABOUT ADDICT CHICK

AMANDA MEREDITH IS A BESTSELLING AUTHOR AND THE VOICE BEHIND *ADDICT CHICK*. SHE IS THE TATTOOED MOM TO A TEENAGER NAMED MASON, A RECOVERING DRUG ADDICT, AND A BADASS CHICK. SHE LOVES JESUS, ROCK FESTIVALS AND IS OBSESSED WITH HER CRAZY DOBERMANS, TEMPEST AND SULLY. SHE LIVES IN *LEXINGTON, KENTUCKY*.

WRITING QUOTES AND TURNING THEM INTO MEMES IS HER NIRVANA. SHE IS AN AVID DIYER AND KNOWS HOW TO USE A MITER SAW AND KREG JIG. (THANKS, MOM!) SHE IS THE KILLER OF ALL PLANTS, DEFINITELY A LITTLE CRAZY, AND TOTALLY AN INFJ. IN A PAST LIFE, SHE WAS AN AMBITIOUS, NOT-VERY-NICE, RELENTLESS OVERACHIEVER IN CORPORATE AMERICA. WHEN SHE IS NOT WRITING, YOU CAN FIND HER WITH HER NOSE BURIED IN A BOOK OR BRIBING HER SPAWN TO SPEND TIME WITH HER.

IN A WORLD WHERE ADDICTION IS STIGMATIZED, AND ADDICTS ARE CONSIDERED A SCAR ON SOCIETY, SHE CHOOSES TO RECOVER OUT-LOUD AND ACROSS SOCIAL MEDIA.

www.AddictChick.com
@AddictChick on all the things!

www.AmethystRecovery.org

IF YOU OR SOMEBODY THAT YOU LOVE IS STRUGGLING WITH SUBSTANCE ABUSE, WE CAN HELP.

www.TheFreedomCenter.com

CALL FOR HELP NOW
855-740-0202

www.ingramcontent.com/pod-product-compliance
Lightning Source LLC
Chambersburg PA
CBHW030903080526
44589CB00010B/130